AUTHENTIC TRANSCRIPTIONS
WITH NOTES AND TABLATURE

M000104694

JOHN FAHEY
GUITAR ANTHOLOGY

Cover Photo: Michael Ochs Archives/Getty Images

Music Transcriptions by Pete Billmann, Jeff Jacobson and Paul Pappas

ISBN 978-1-4950-3603-3

HAL•LEONARD®
CORPORATION
7777 W. BLUEMOUND RD. P.O. BOX 13819 MILWAUKEE, WI 53213

In Australia Contact:
Hal Leonard Australia Pty. Ltd.
4 Lentara Court
Cheltenham, Victoria, 3192 Australia
Email: ausadmin@halleonard.com.au

Visit Hal Leonard Online at
www.halleonard.com

AMERICAN PRIMITIVE GUITAR

One of the last, great pioneers of guitar exploration, the late John Aloysius Fahey (1939–2001) was the grandfather of instrumental acoustic fingerstyle guitar. For over four decades, Fahey's vast output of raw, imaginative, deeply beautiful, and sometimes bone-chilling guitar compositions have inspired legions of followers, including such disparate artists as Pete Townshend, Leo Kottke, Beck, Thurston Moore, and Jim O'Rourke, not to mention countless bedroom fingerpickers across the planet.

More than just a self-taught guitarist, Fahey was a musicologist, composer, record collector, writer, independent record label owner, painter, thinker, provocateur, visionary, and iconoclast. These attributes helped inform his unique sound, often infused with a variety of styles reaching far beyond the anchor of the blues he so loved, incorporating folk, classical, avant-garde, psychedelic, rock, jazz, country, bluegrass, world music, and more. John viewed the guitar as an orchestra in itself, regularly employing counterpoint and alternating bass as his main compositional vehicles. Someone later coined Fahey's style "American Primitive Guitar," reflecting the untrained, exploratory nature of his approach, derived from his study of American roots music.

Eighteen of his works live on in this *John Fahey Guitar Anthology*, a definitive collection of note-for-note guitar transcriptions presented in both standard notation and tablature, covering his most iconic recordings from the 1960s and '70s. Fahey recorded multiple versions of several early pieces (sometimes three or four, and even with alternate titles), so to avoid confusion, the source album will be noted with each song in this collection, as well as in the following Discography.

Many of this book's corresponding recordings can be found on the excellent John Fahey compilation albums released in the 1990s, in particular, *The Legend of Blind Joe Death* and *Death Chants, Breakdowns & Military Waltzes*. But to create even further confusion, both of these albums include *two* versions of most of the songs—the originals and the "updated" recordings he produced a few years later. In the Discography, these are designated as "1" or "2," respectively, so it is clear which version each transcription is based upon.

Before you begin your guitar adventure, it is helpful to note a few things about Fahey's technique. He used a thumbpick and two fingerpicks (on the index and middle fingers), much like a banjo player. Picks are not necessary to learn the songs, but they will help in emulating the Fahey sound, if so desired. Otherwise, fingernails will do just fine. Alternating bass notes played with the thumb are used throughout these pieces, and often repeated with variations. Though Fahey's technique was far from traditional, you can generally assign the thumb to the bottom three low strings, and the fingers to the top three high strings. The key to most of Fahey's material is learning the pick-hand patterns; once you can get them engrained in your fingers, you'll be off and pickin'.

DISCOGRAPHY

The Legend of Blind Joe Death (1996, Takoma – compilation album)
- "Desperate Man Blues" (2)
- "In Christ There Is No East or West" (2)
- "John Henry" (1)
- "Poor Boy, Long Ways from Home" (2)
- "Sligo River Blues" (2)
- "Sun's Gonna Shine in My Backdoor Someday Blues" (2)

Death Chants, Breakdowns & Military Waltzes (1996, Takoma – compilation album)
- "Dance of the Inhabitants of the Palace of King Phillip of Spain"
- "Some Summer Day" (2)
- "Spanish Dance" (2)
- "Sunflower River Blues" (2)
- "When the Springtime Comes Again" (2)

The Transfiguration of Blind Joe Death (1965, Takoma)
- "Brenda's Blues"
- "Tell Her to Come Back Home"

The Yellow Princess (1968, Vanguard)
- "The Yellow Princess"

America (1971, Takoma)
- "America"

Old Fashioned Love (1975, Takoma)
- "The Assassination of Stephan Grossman"
- "Jaya Shiva Shankarah" (duet with Woodrow Mann)

Live in Tasmania (1981, Takoma)
- "Steamboat Gwine 'Round de Bend"

America
Written by John Fahey

Drop D tuning:
(low to high) D-A-D-G-B-E

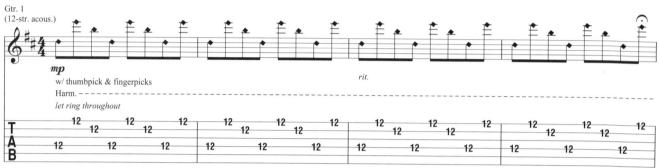

*Chord symbols reflect implied harmony.

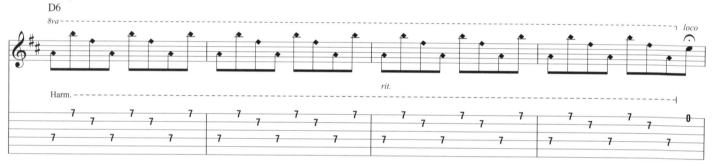

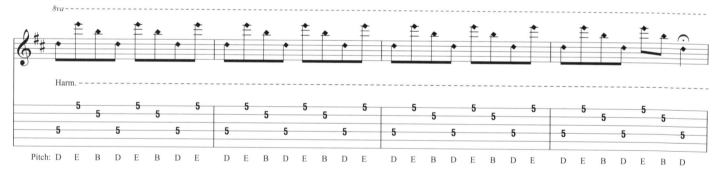

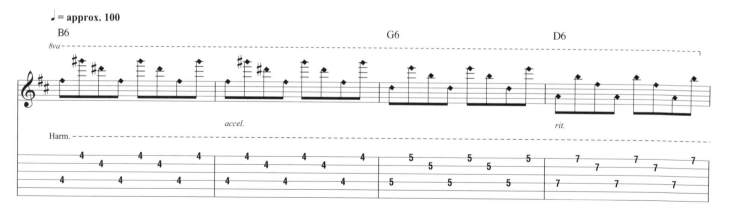

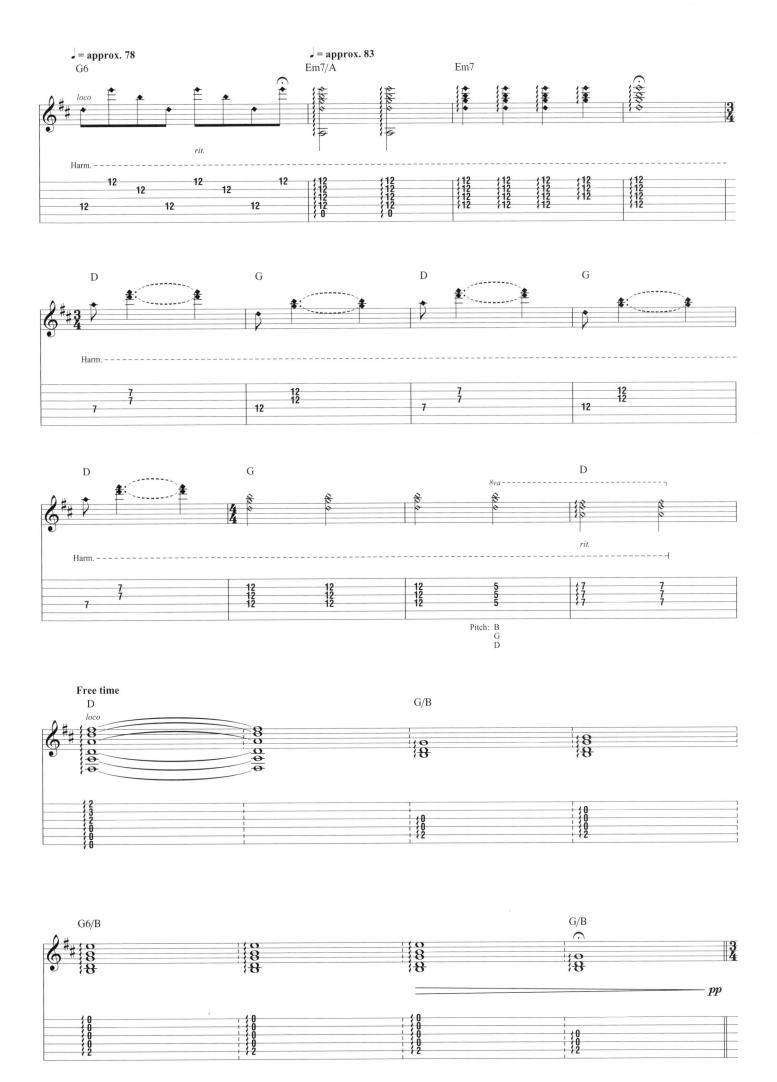

B

Moderately slow ♩ = 70

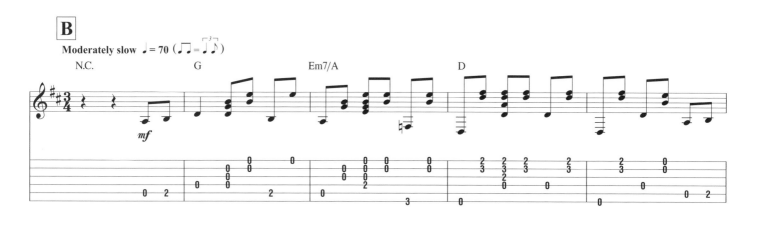

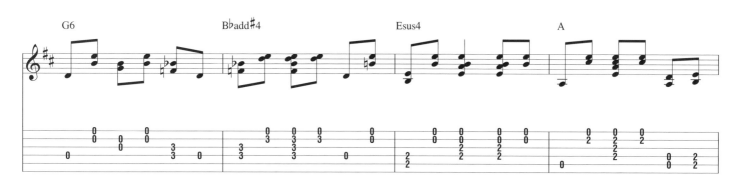

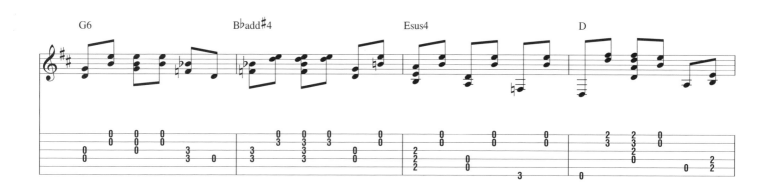

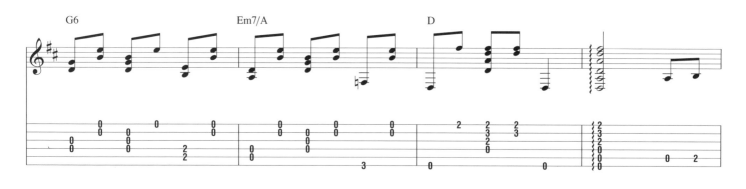

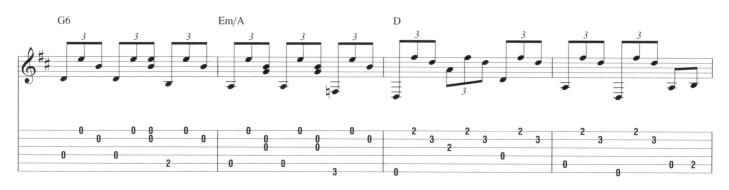

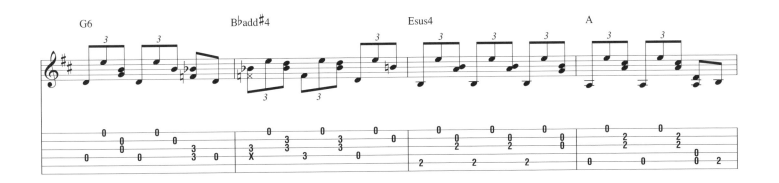

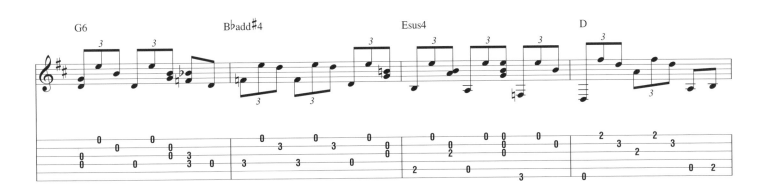

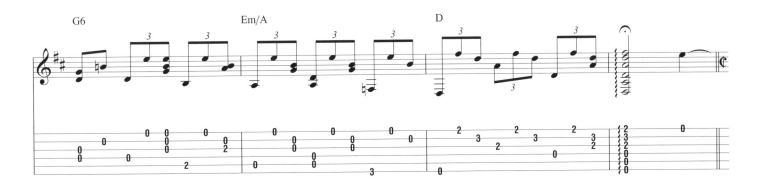

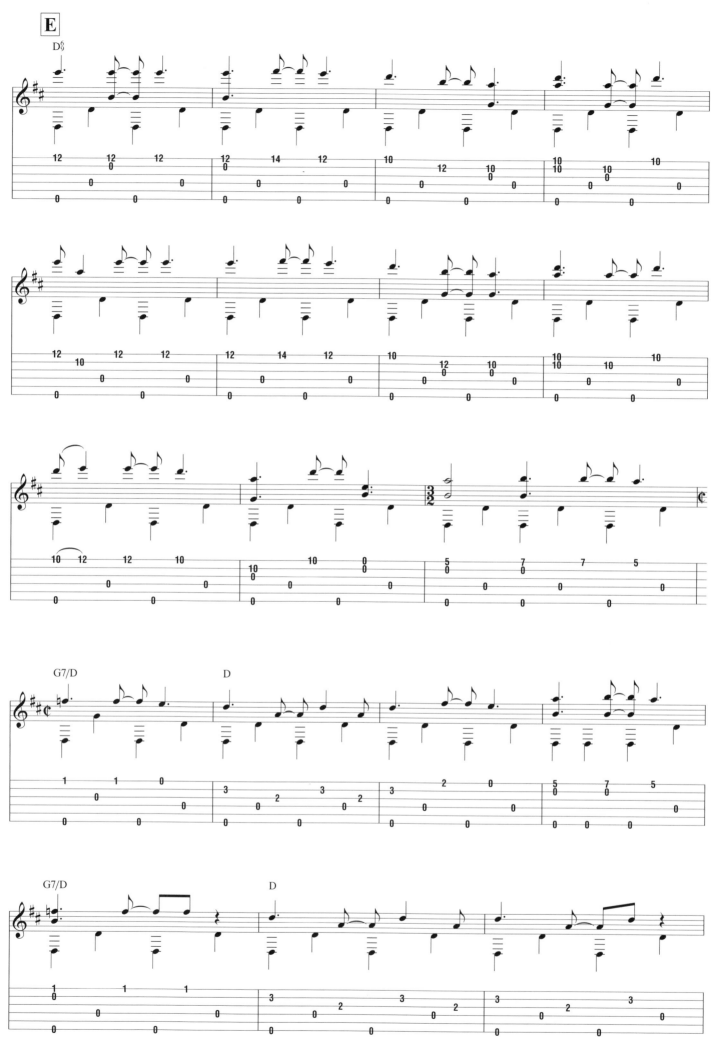

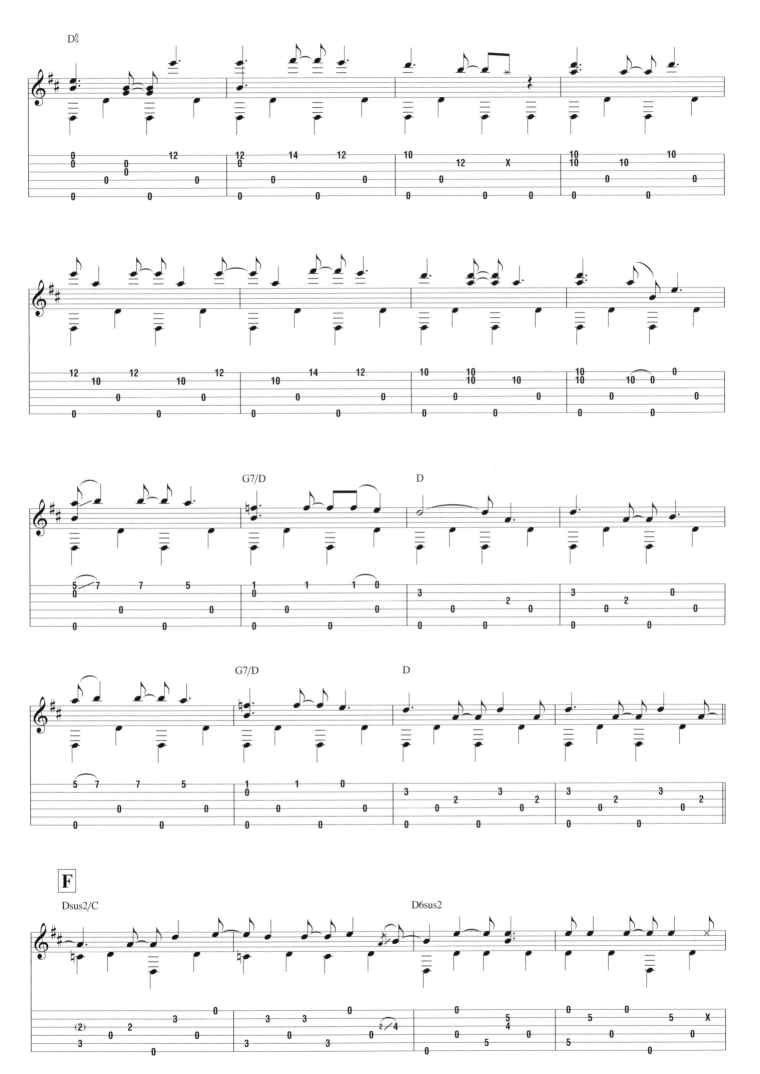

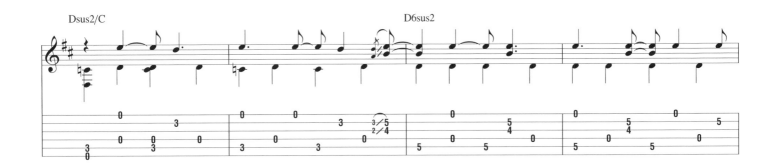

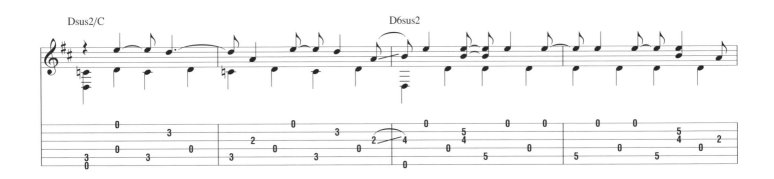

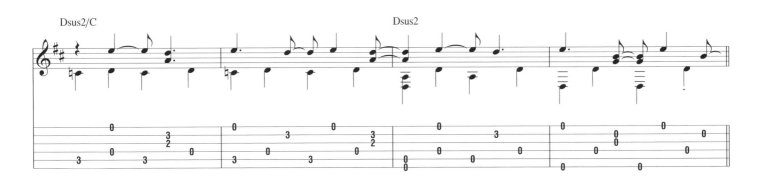

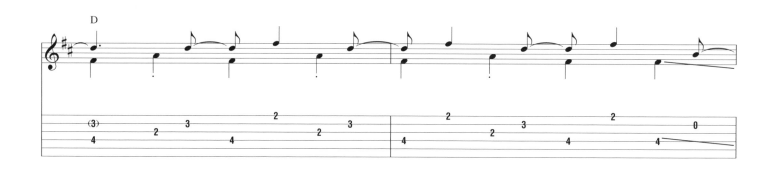

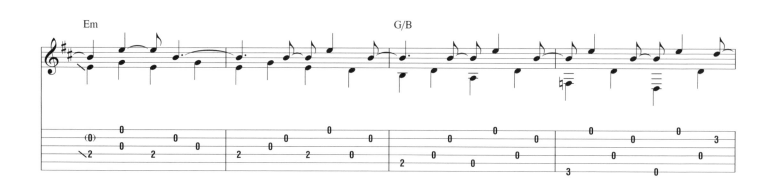

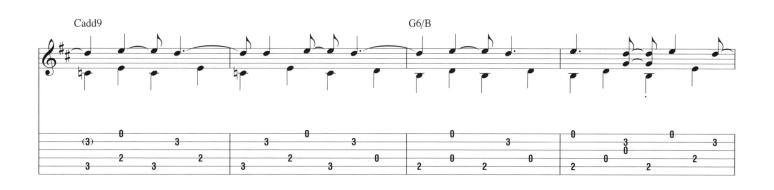

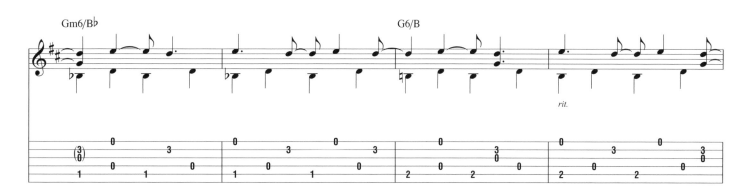

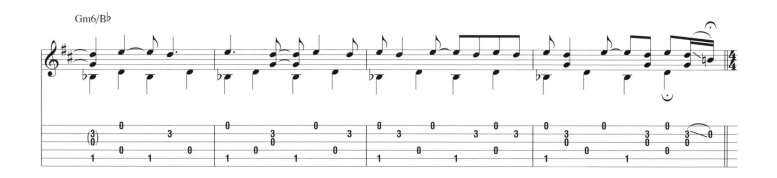

J

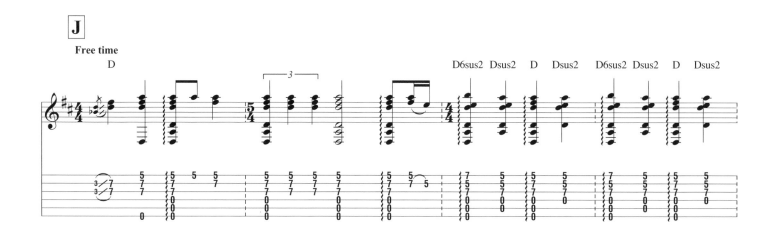

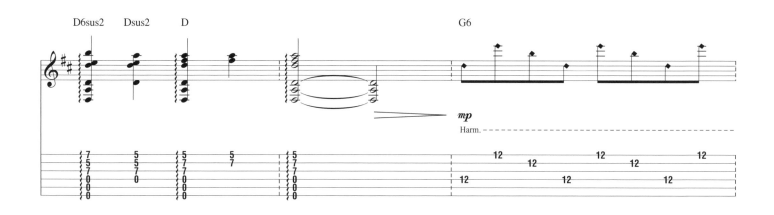

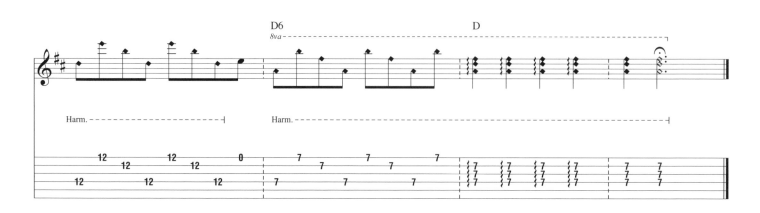

from *Death Chants, Breakdowns & Military Waltzes*

When the Springtime Comes Again

Written by John Fahey

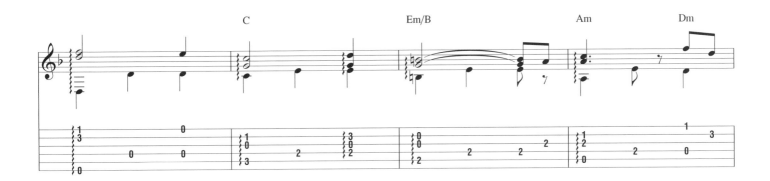

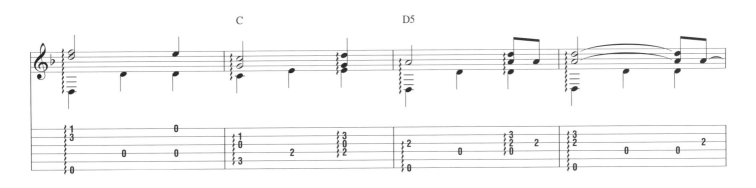

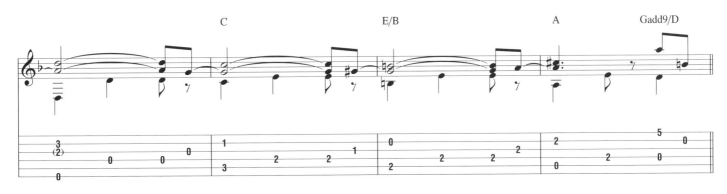

*Both downstemmed notes plucked w/ thumb.

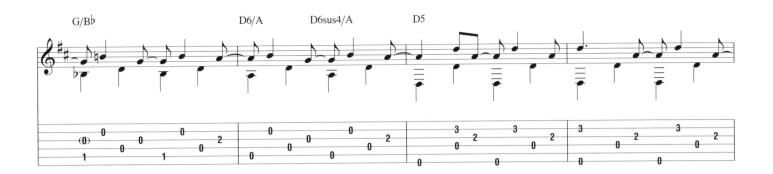

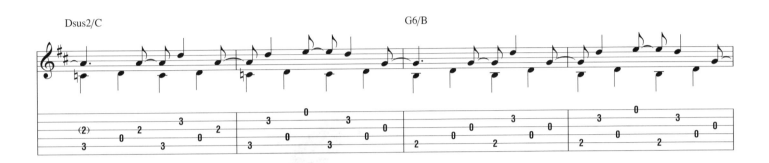

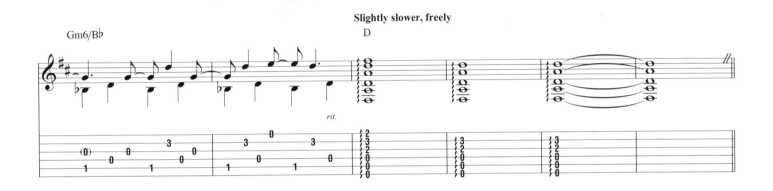

I

Moderately slow ♩ = 96

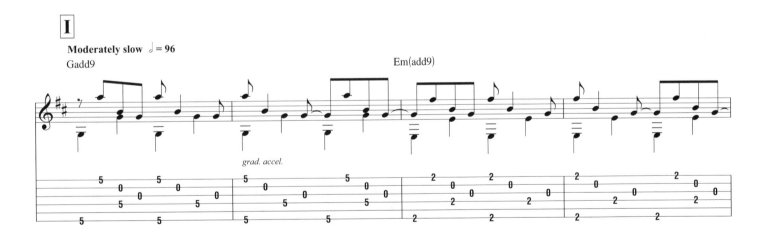

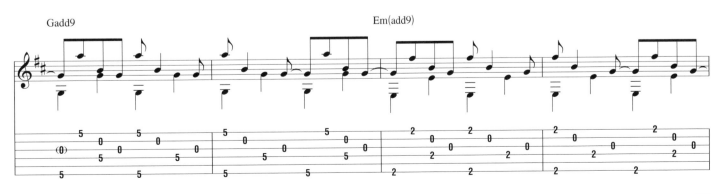

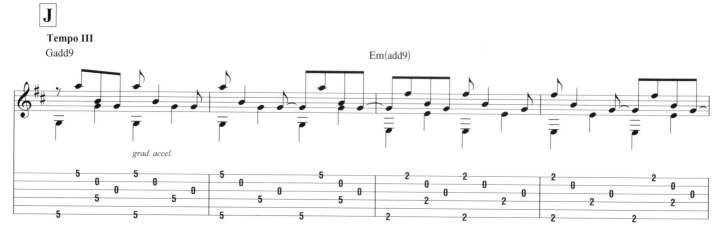

24

Tempo II

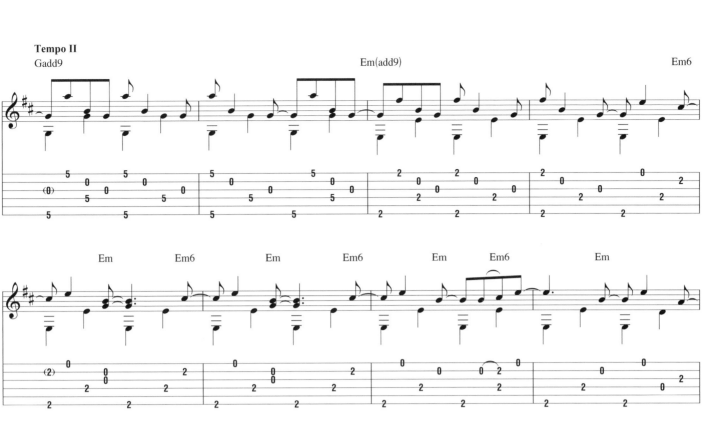

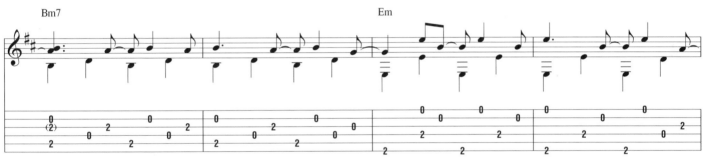

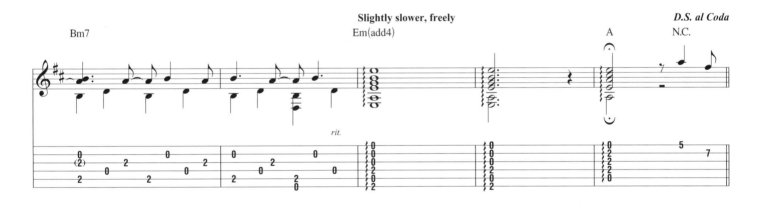

Slightly slower, freely

D.S. al Coda

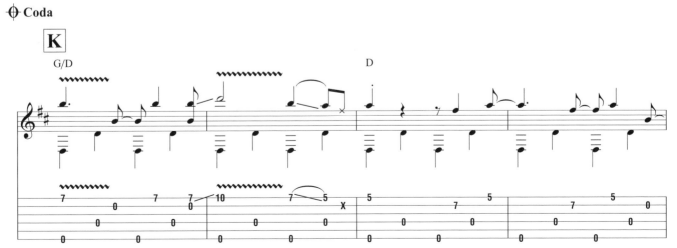

✛ **Coda**

25

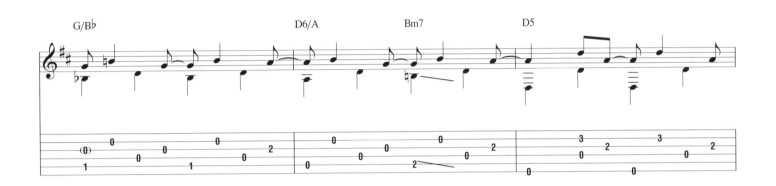

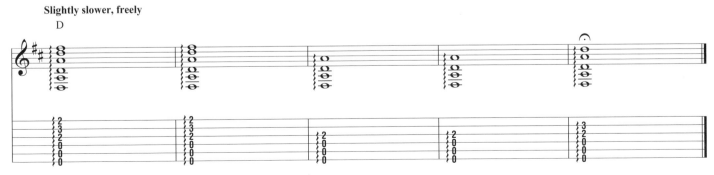

from *Old Fashioned Love*

The Assassination of Stephan Grossman

Written by John Fahey

*To play along with recording, tune down 1/4 step.
**Chord symbols reflect implied harmony.

***T = Thumb on 6th string

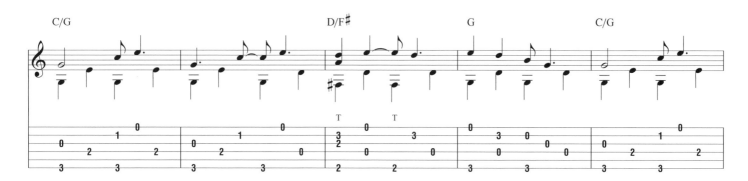

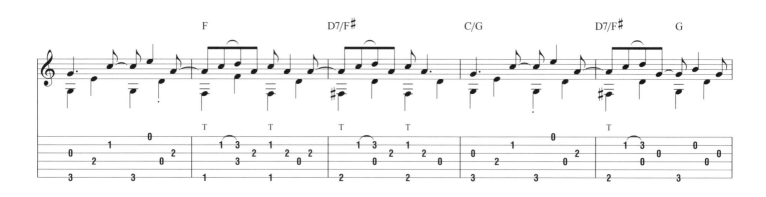

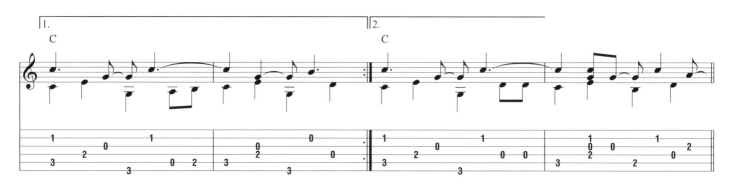

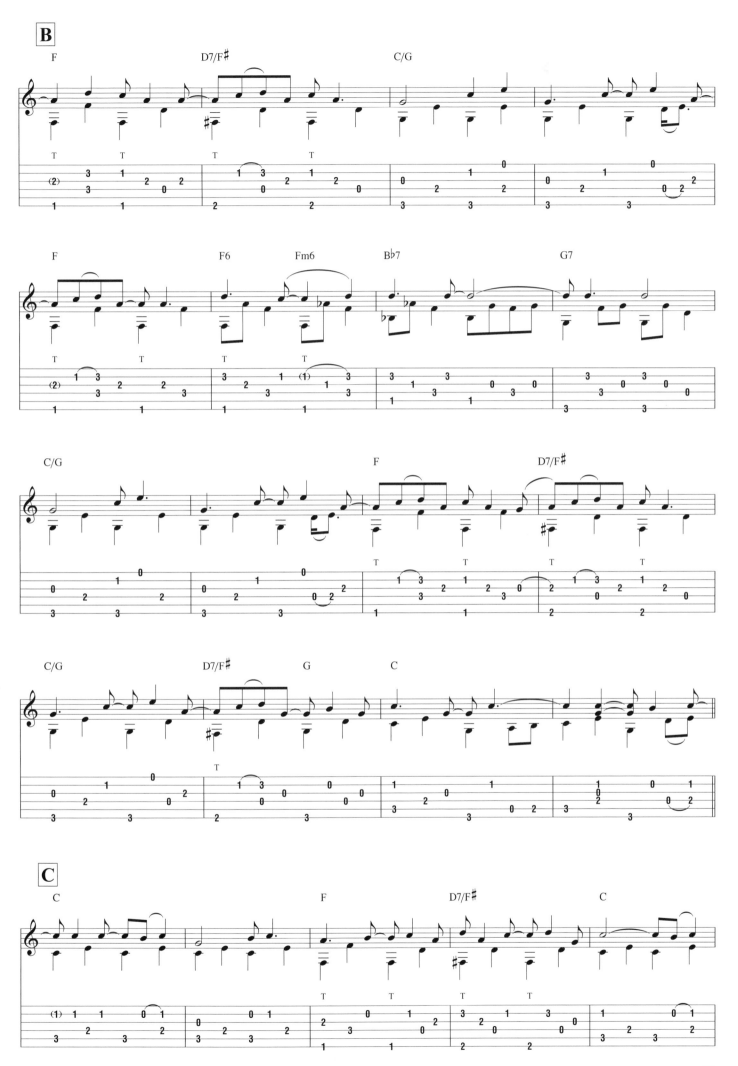

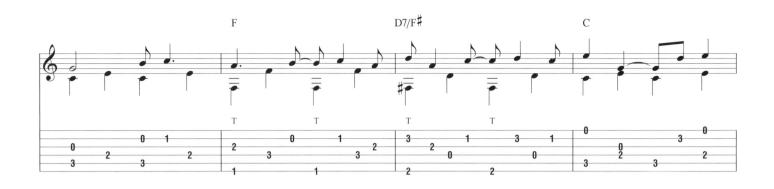

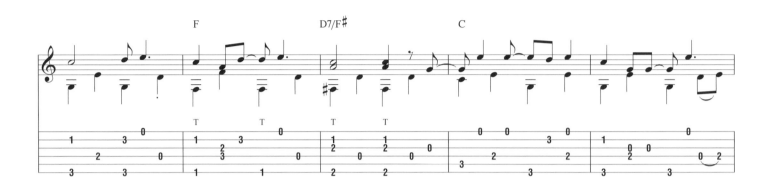

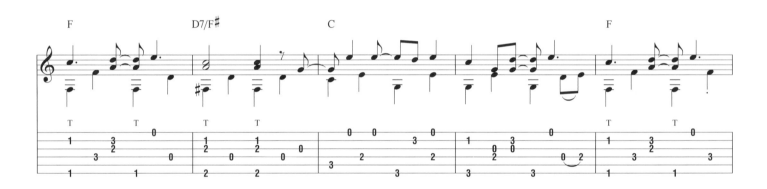

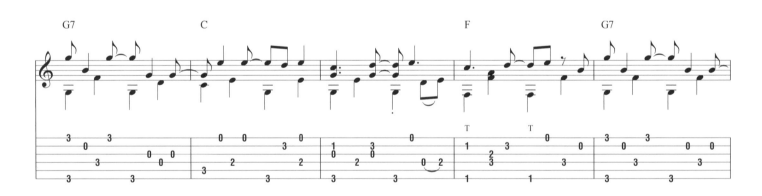

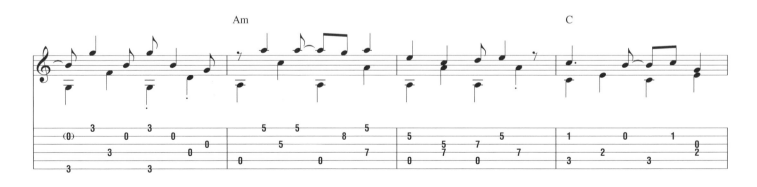

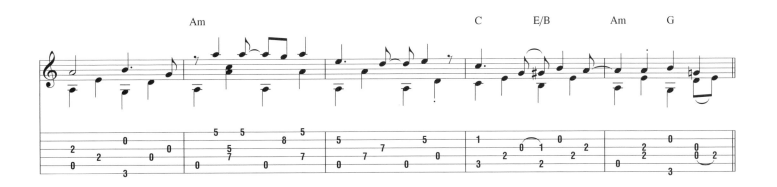

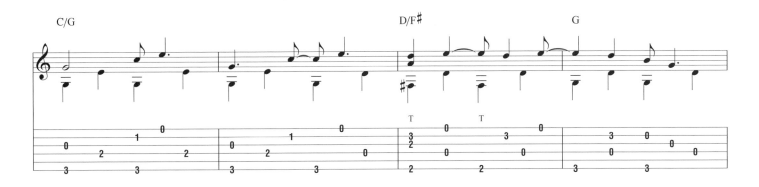

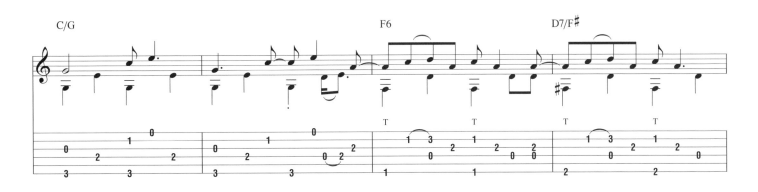

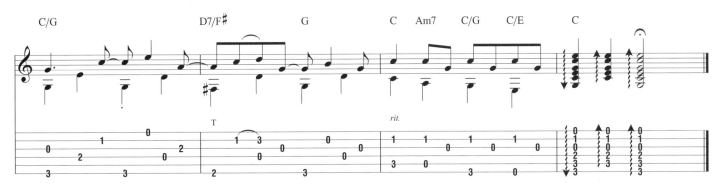

Brenda's Blues

Written by John Fahey

Capo III

*Symbols in parentheses represent chord names respective to capoed guitar.
Symbols above reflect actual sounding chords. Capoed fret is "0" in tab.
Chord symbols reflect basic harmony.

**T = Thumb on 6th string

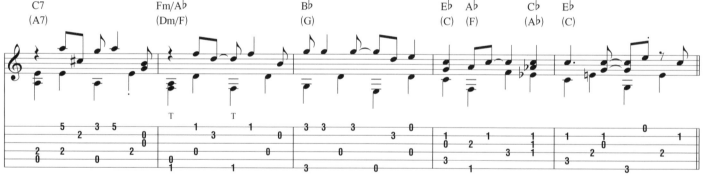

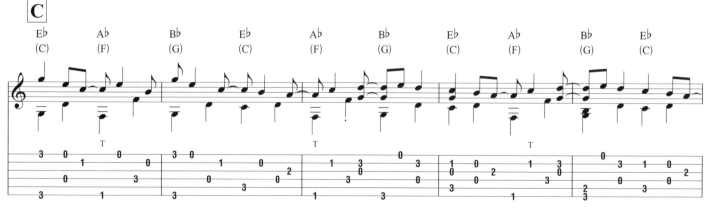

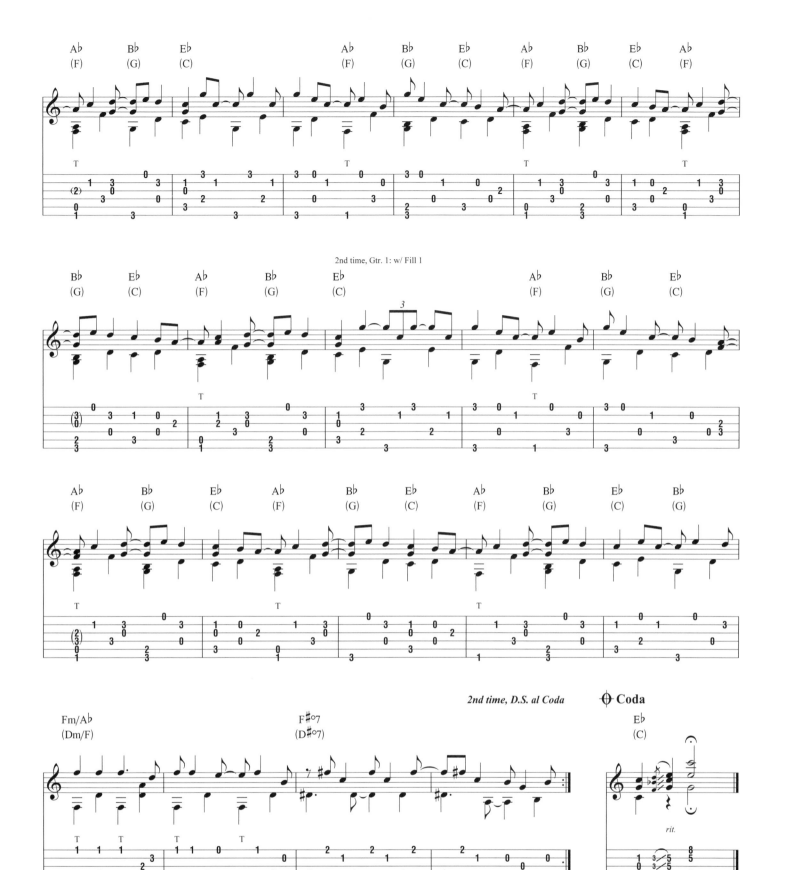

2nd time, Gtr. 1: w/ Fill 1

2nd time, D.S. al Coda $\oplus$ **Coda**

from *Death Chants, Breakdowns & Military Waltzes*

Dance of the Inhabitants of the Palace of King Phillip of Spain

Written by John Fahey

35

Desperate Man Blues

Written by John Fahey

Open G tuning, down 1/2 step:
(low to high) ↑G♭-G♭-D♭-G♭-B♭-D♭

A

Moderately ♩ = 98

*Chord symbols reflect implied harmony.

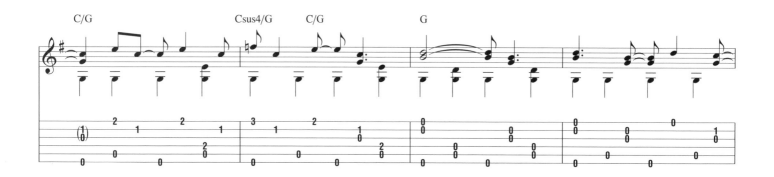

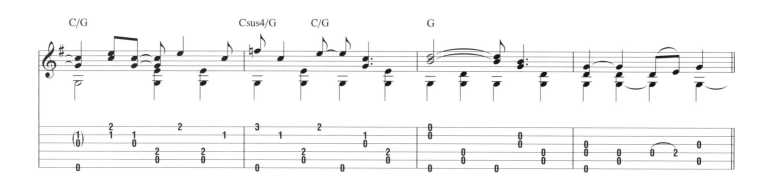

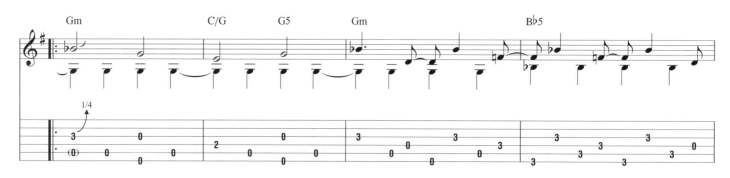

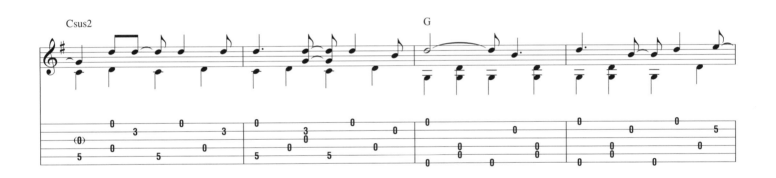

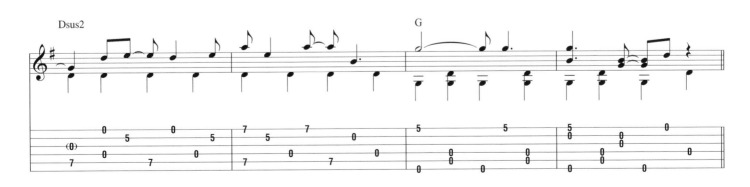

C/G   G5

C/G   G5

2nd time, Gtr. 1: w/ Fill 1
D   D7   C   G5

To Coda 2 ⊕

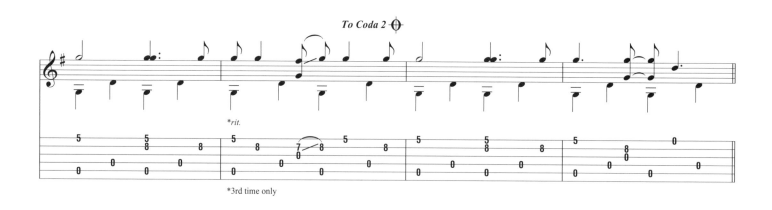

*rit.

*3rd time only

Fill 1
Gtr. 1

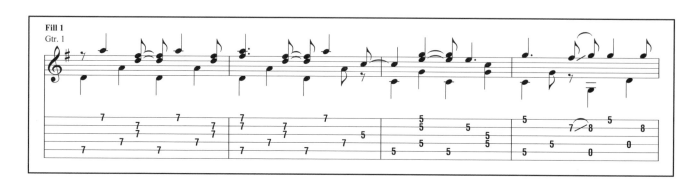

To Coda 1 ⊕

D.S. al Coda 1
(take repeat)

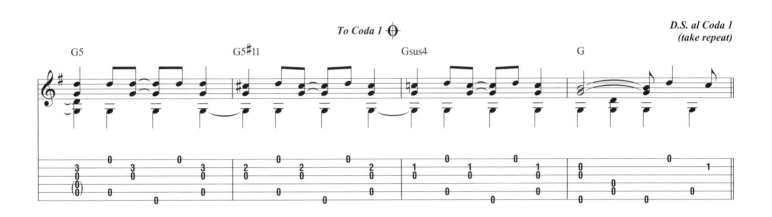

⊕ **Coda 1**

D.S.S. al Coda 2

⊕ **Coda 2**

from *The Legend of Blind Joe Death*

In Christ There Is No East or West

Traditional
Arranged and Adapted by John Fahey

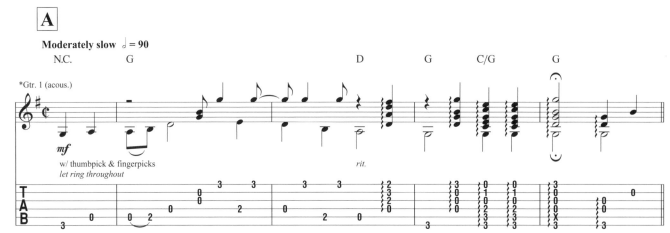

*To play along with recording, tune up 1/4 step.

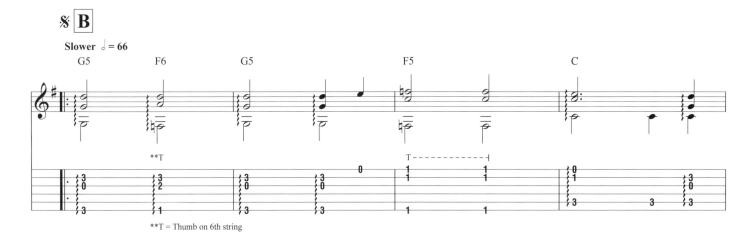

**T = Thumb on 6th string

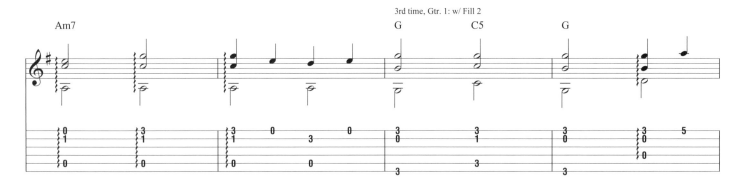

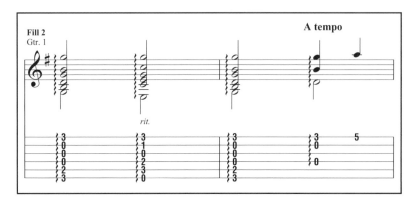

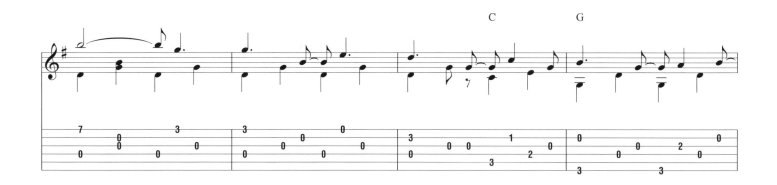

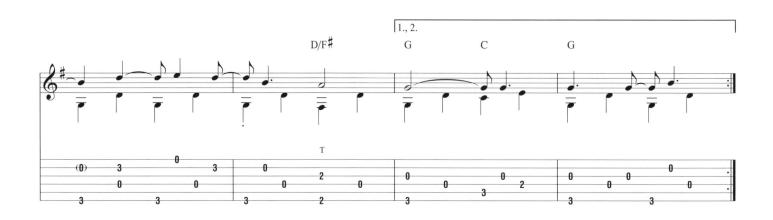

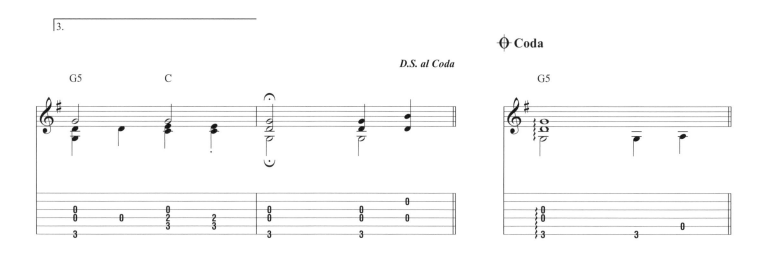

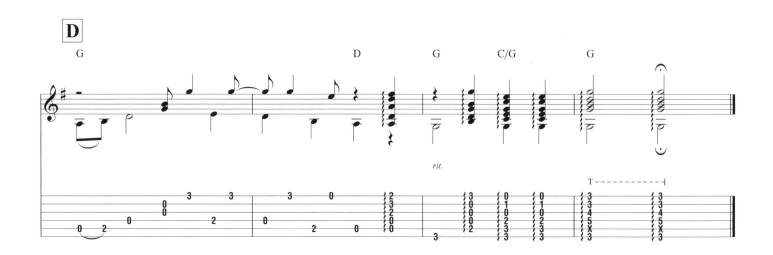

from *Old Fashioned Love*

Jaya Shiva Shankarah

Arranged by John Fahey

Gtr. 1: Open C tuning:
(low to high) C-G-C-G-C-E

*John Fahey
**Slight shuffle feel.

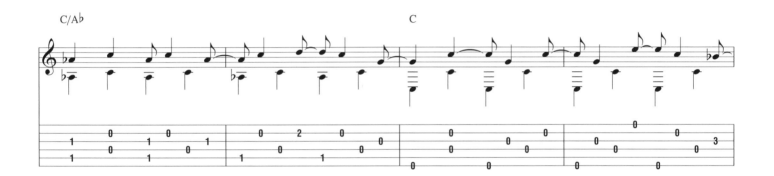

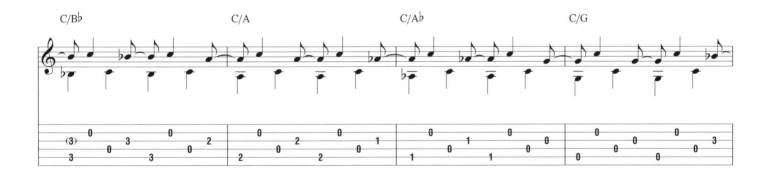

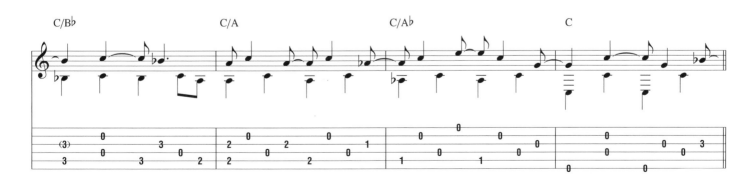

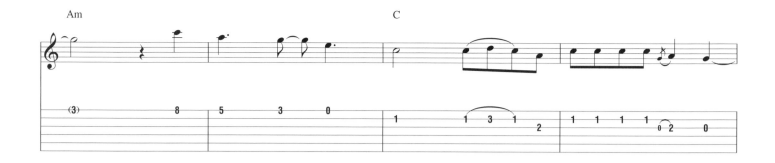

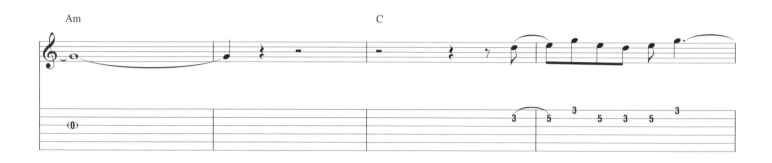

D.S. al Coda 1
(take 2nd ending)

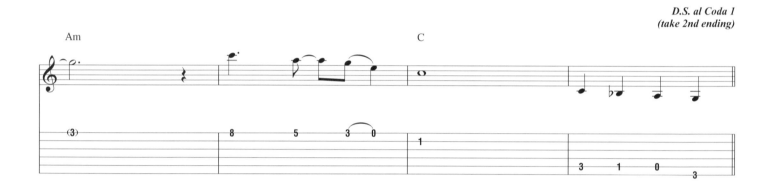

Coda 1

D.S. al Coda 2
(take 2nd ending)

Coda 2

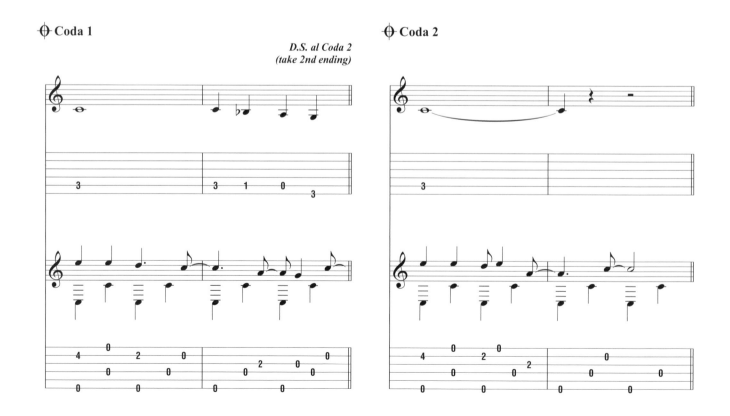

52

*Disregard initial upstemmed tie.

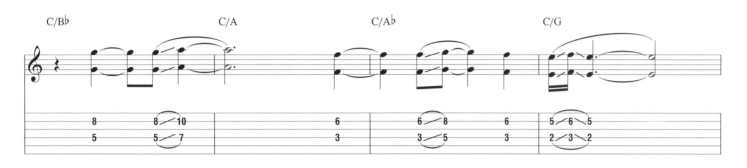

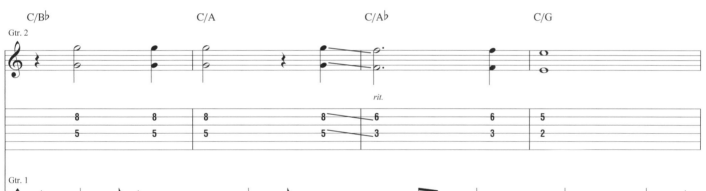

*Disregard initial upstemmed tied note.

I

*Gtr. 1: w/ Riff A (1st 12 meas.)

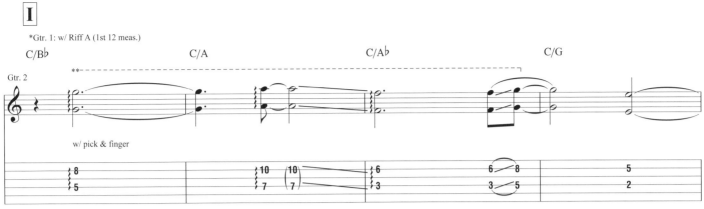

*w/ grad rit. & decresc., last 8 meas.

**Played behind the beat.

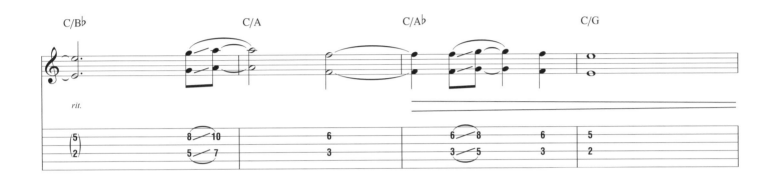

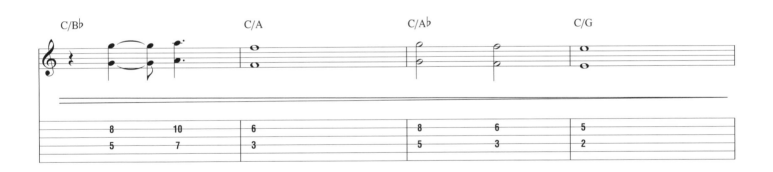

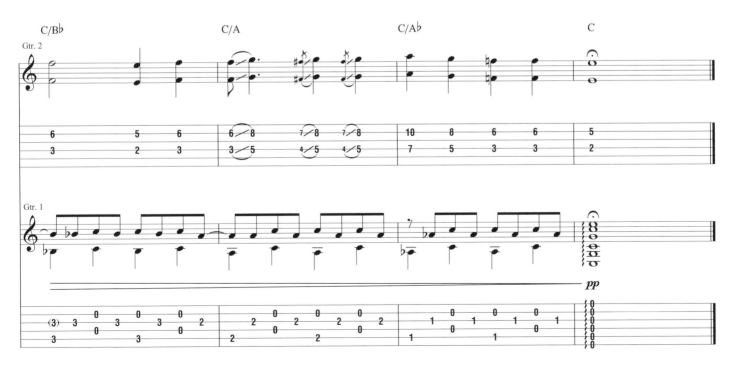

from *The Legend of Blind Joe Death*
John Henry
Arranged by John Fahey

*Slight shuffle feel.
**Chord symbols reflect basic harmony.

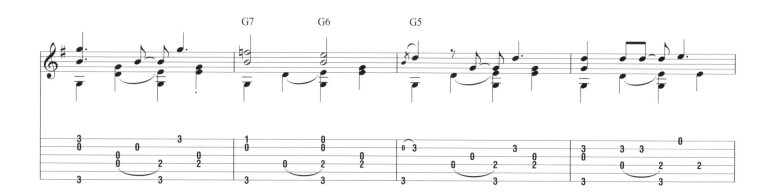

2nd-5th times, Gtr. 1: w/ Fill 1

G(#9)

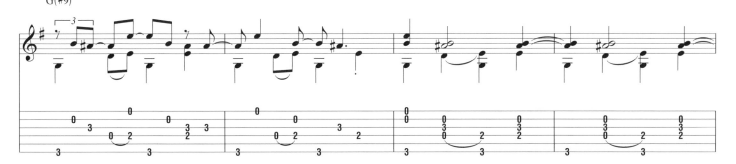

To Coda ⊕

G

Play 4 times

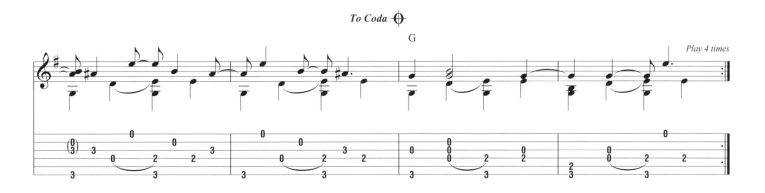

B

G

G7   G6   G5

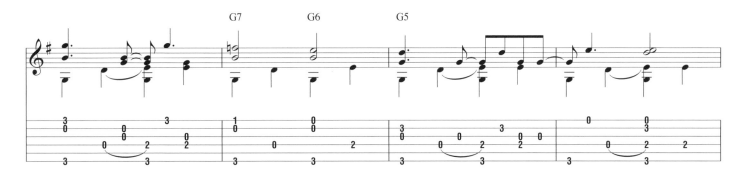

Fill 1
Gtr. 1

from *The Legend of Blind Joe Death*
Poor Boy, Long Ways from Home
Arranged by John Fahey

Open D tuning:
(low to high) D-A-D-F#-A-D

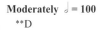

*To play along with recording, tune up 1/4 step.
**Chord symbols reflect basic harmony.

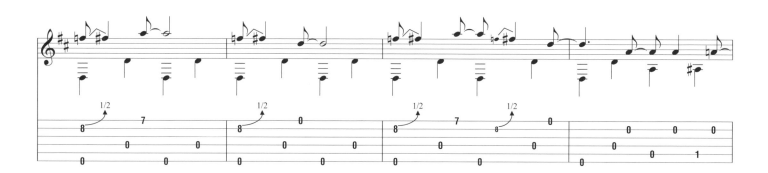

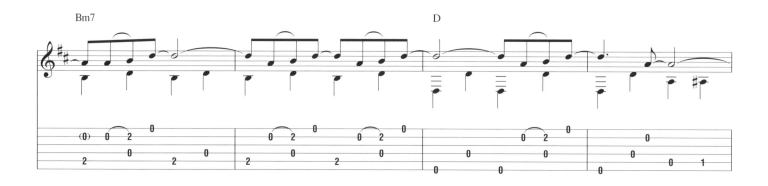

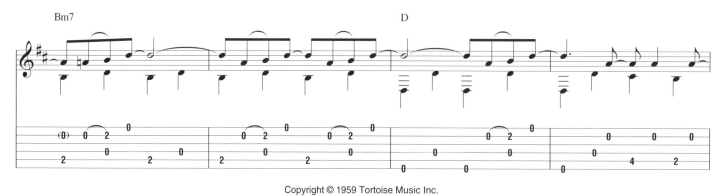

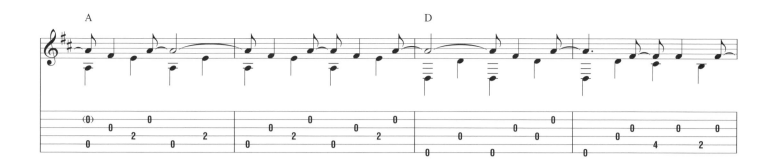

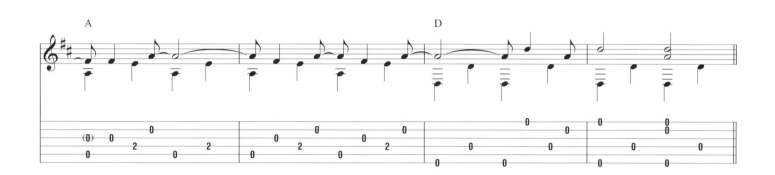

B

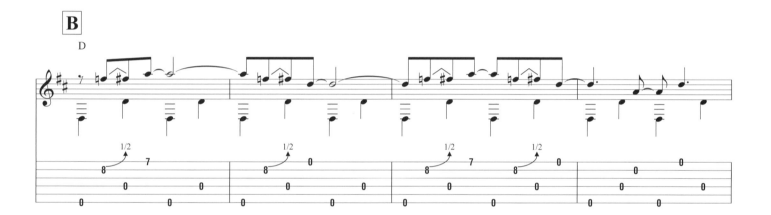

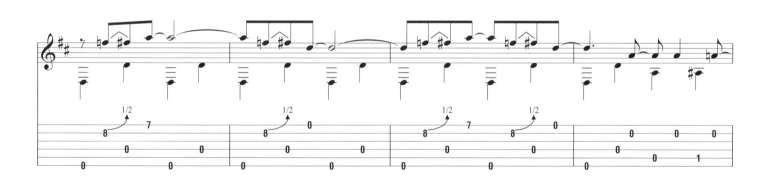

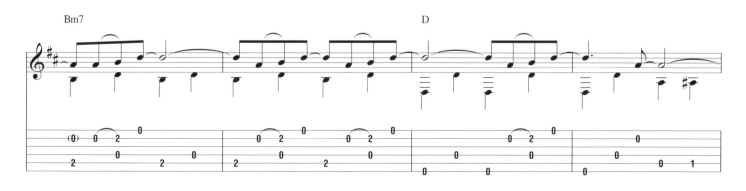

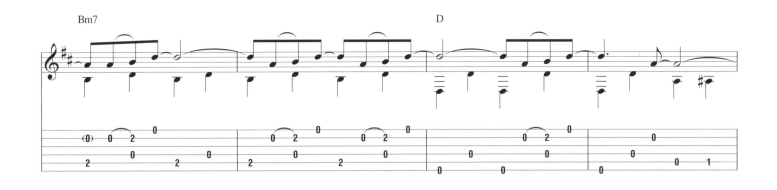

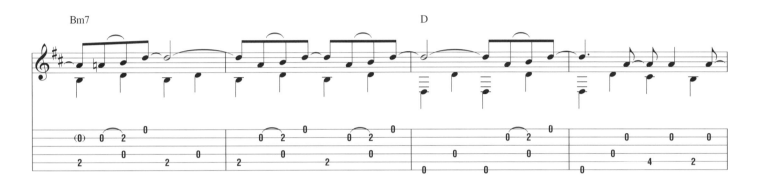

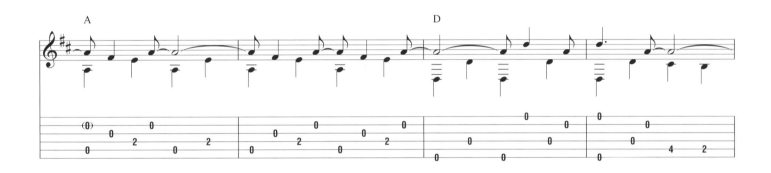

D

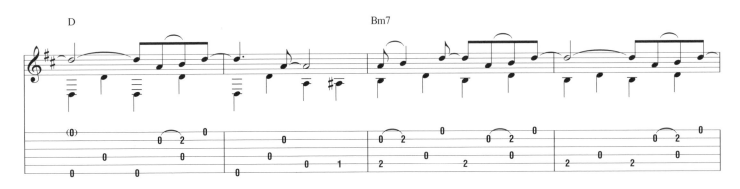

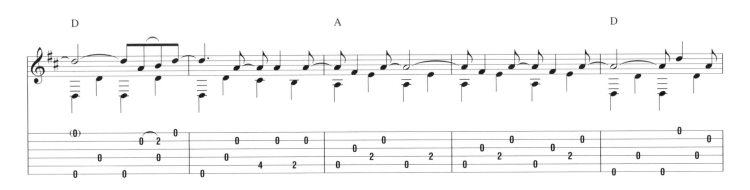

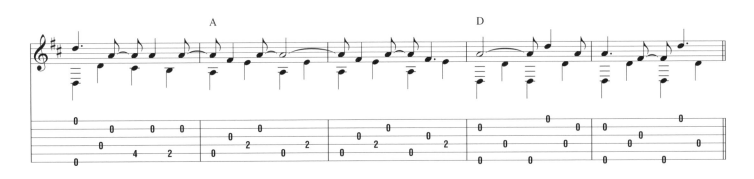

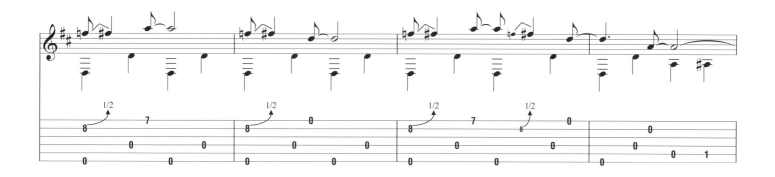

Bm7   D

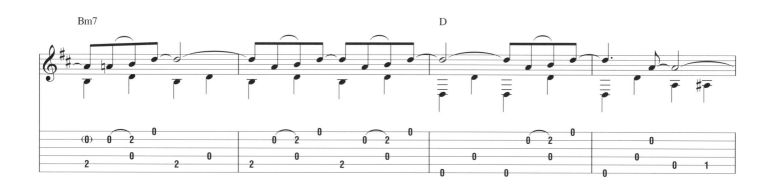

Bm7   D

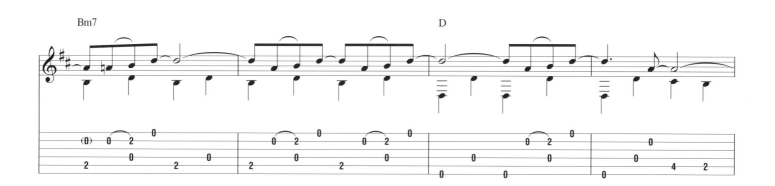

A   D

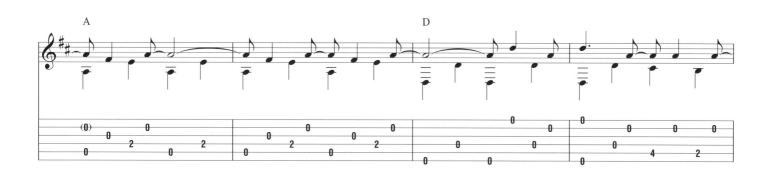

A   D

rit.

from *The Legend of Blind Joe Death*
Sligo River Blues

Written by John Fahey

*Chord symbols reflect basic harmony.

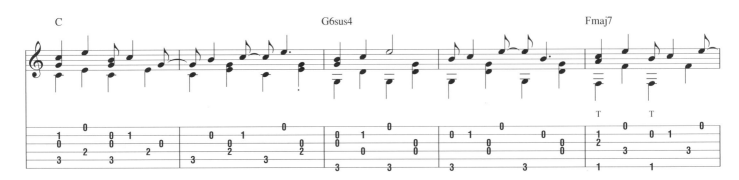

C

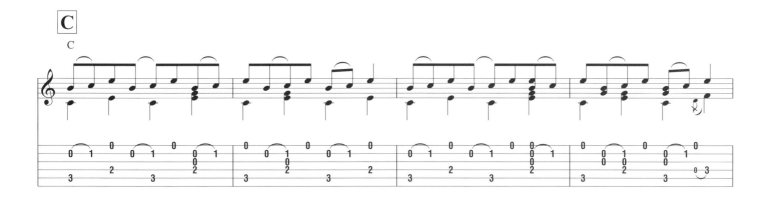

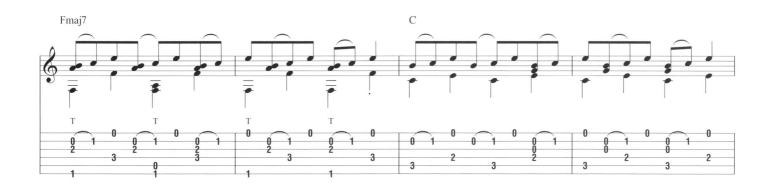

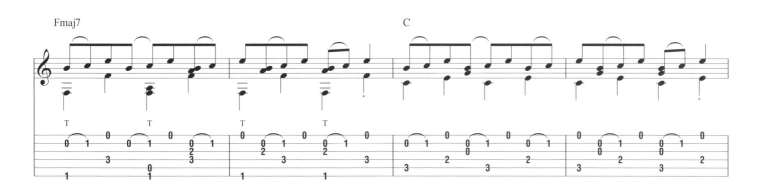

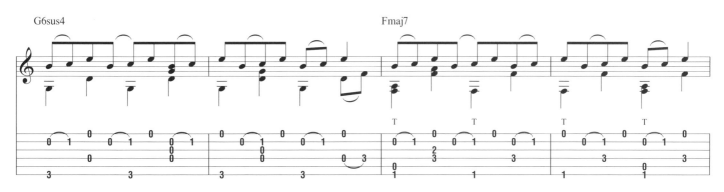

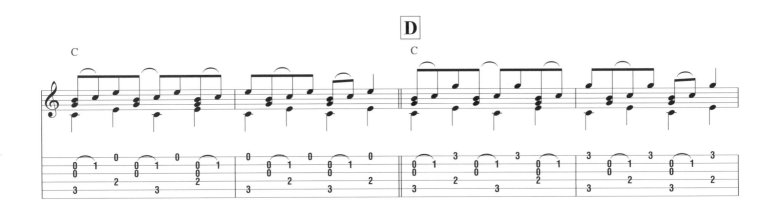

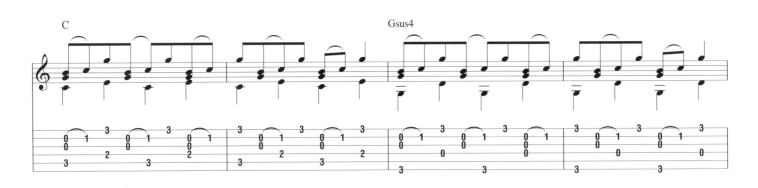

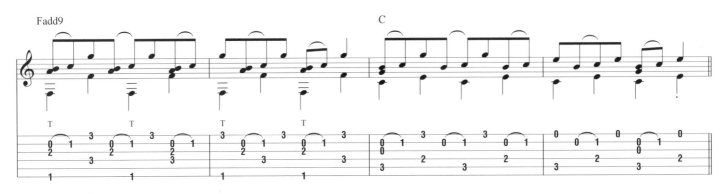

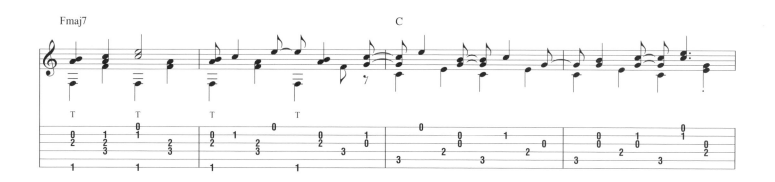

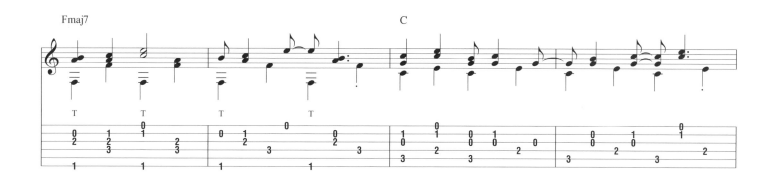

from *Death Chants, Breakdowns & Military Waltzes*

Some Summer Day

Written by John Fahey

*Chord symbols reflect basic harmony.

**T = Thumb on 6th string

***Both downstemmed notes
plucked w/ thumb (throughout).

from *Death Chants, Breakdowns & Military Waltzes*

Spanish Dance

Written by John Fahey

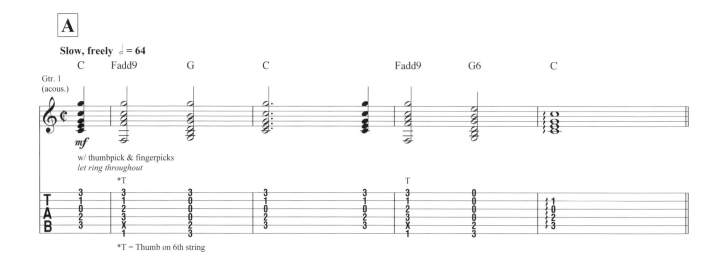

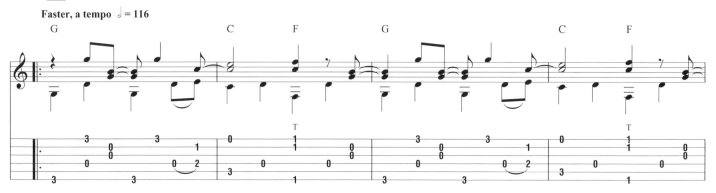

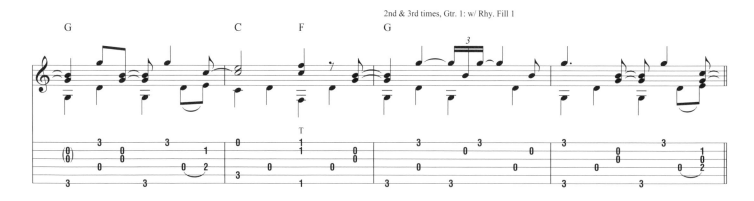

2nd & 3rd times, Gtr. 1: w/ Rhy. Fill 1

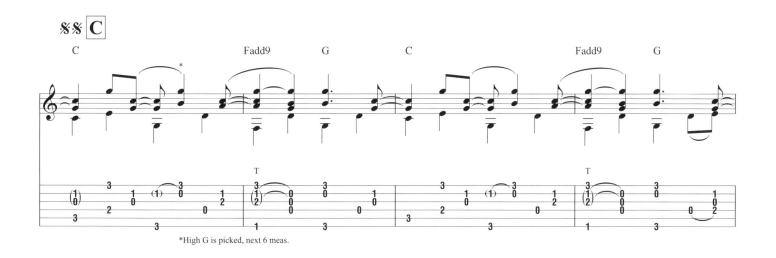

*High G is picked, next 6 meas.

To Coda 1 ⊕

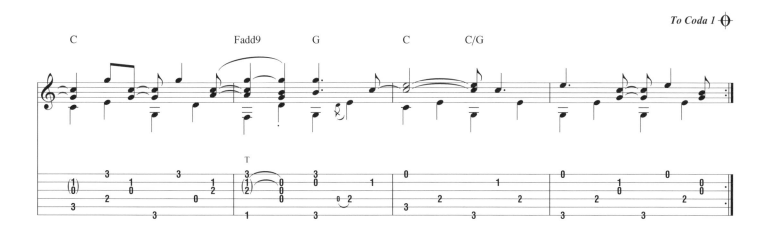

2nd time, Gtr. 1: w/ Rhy. Fill 2

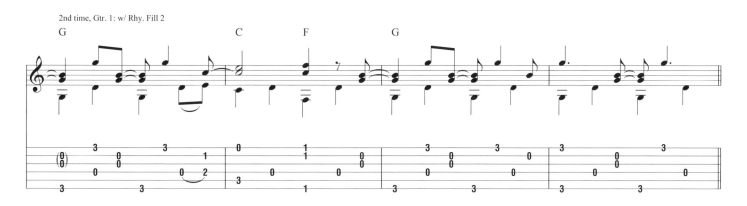

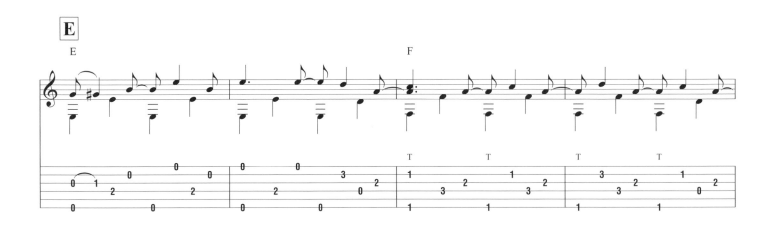

To Coda 2 ⊕

D.S. al Coda 1
(no repeat)

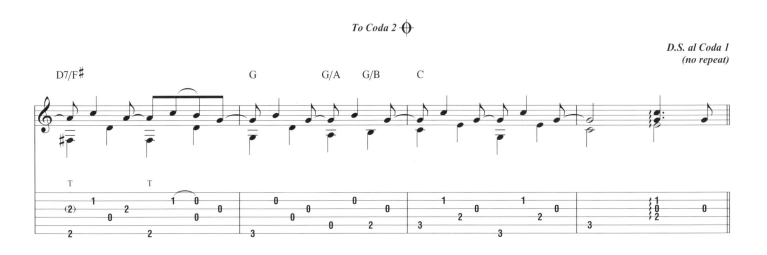

⊕ **Coda 1**

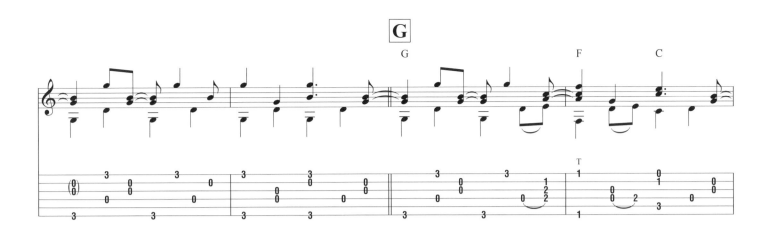

Coda 2

D.S.S. al Coda 2
(no repeat)

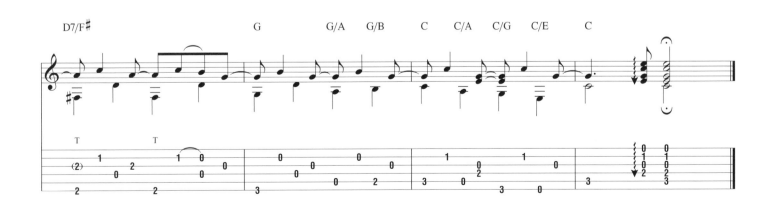

Steamboat Gwine 'Round de Bend

Written by John Fahey

Open G tuning:
(low to high) D-G-D-G-B-D

*Gtr. 1
(acous.)

mp

w/ thumbpick & fingerpicks
w/ slide
let ring throughout

*Lap steel gtr. arr. for gtr.
To play along with recording, tune up 1/4 step.

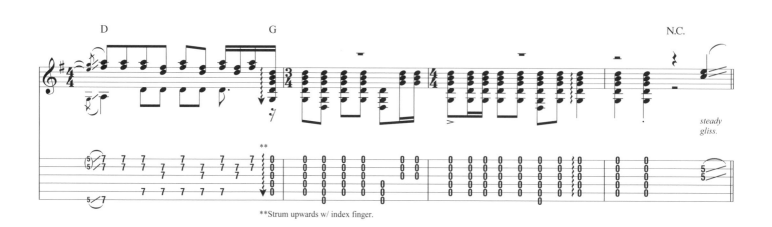

**Strum upwards w/ index finger.

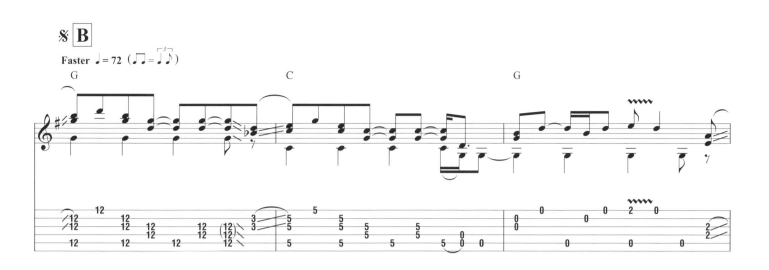

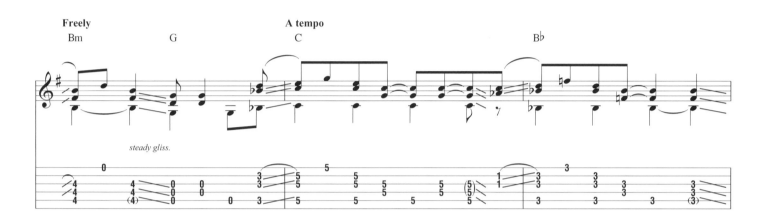

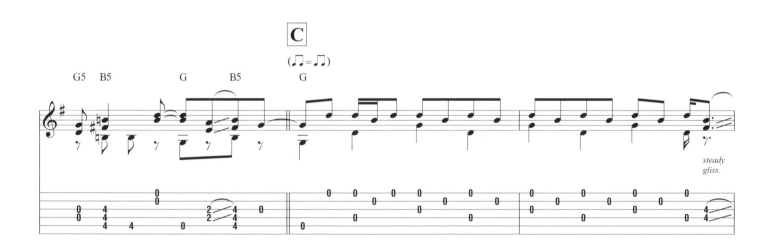

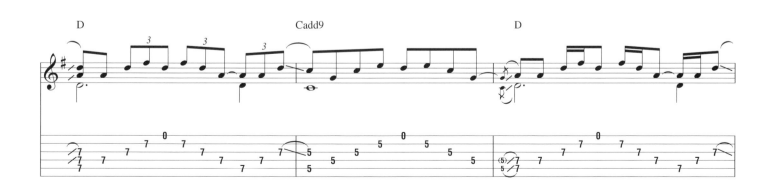

*Both notes plucked w/ thumb.

D

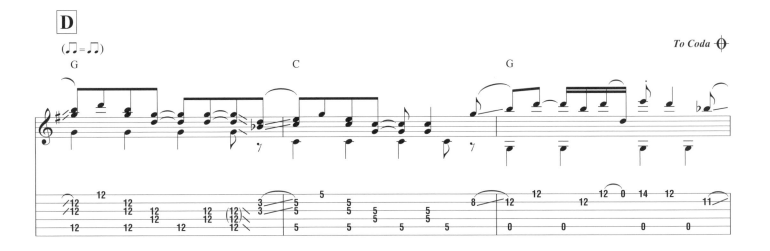

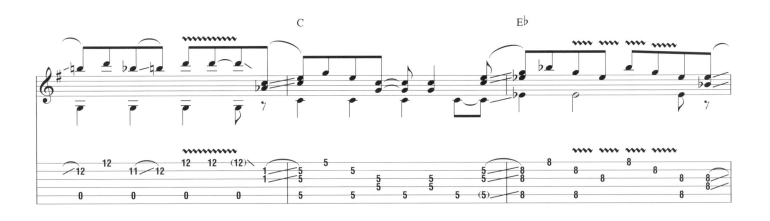

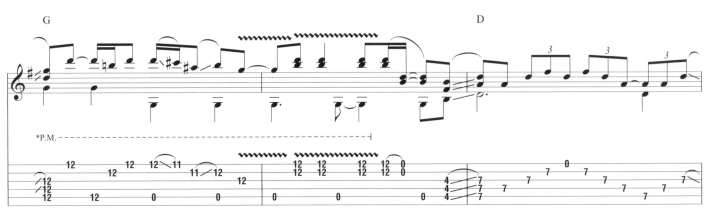

*Refers to downstemmed notes only.

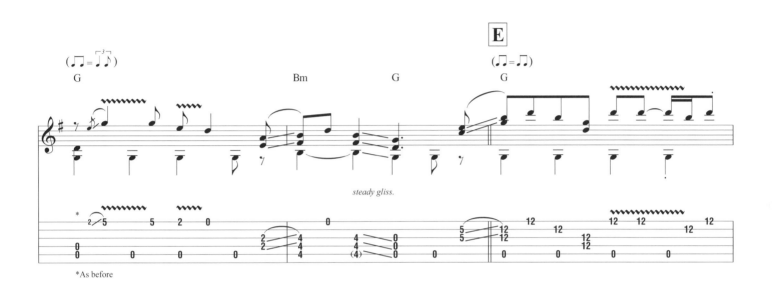

*As before

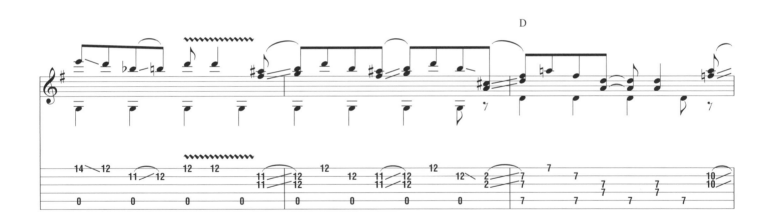

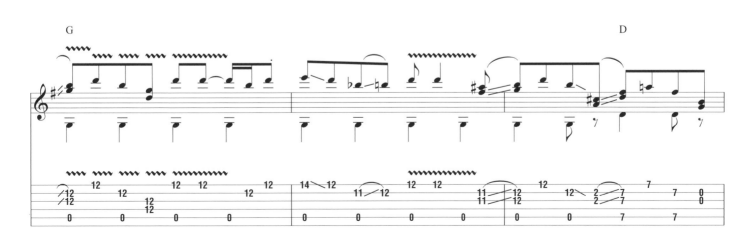

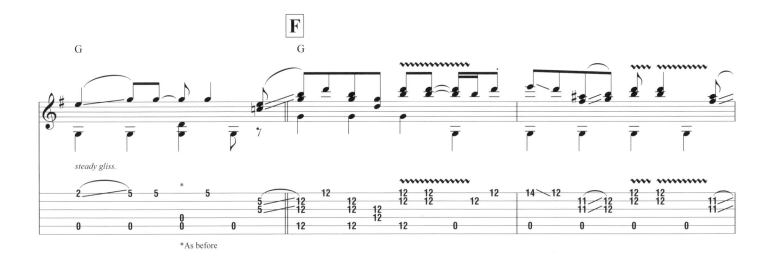

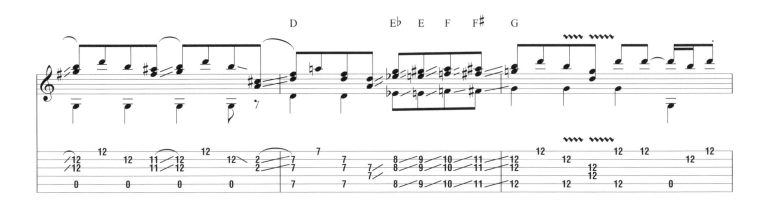

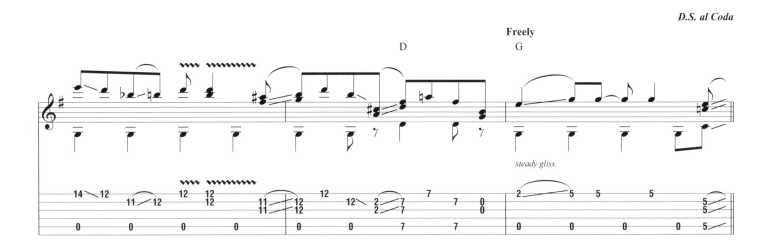

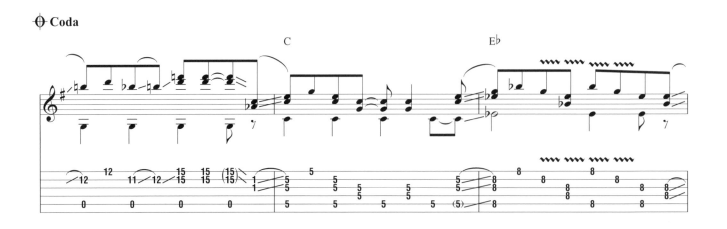

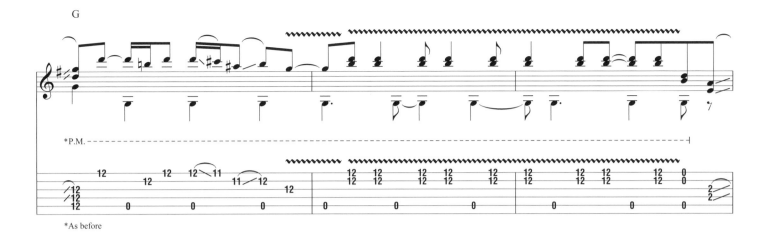

*P.M. - |

*As before

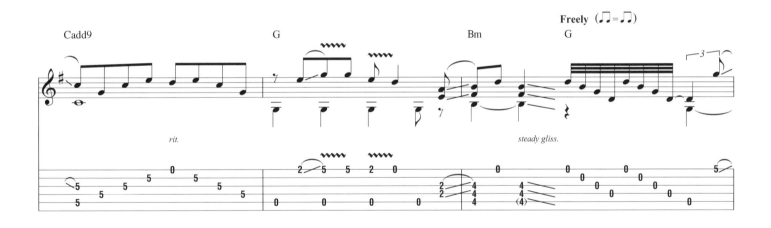

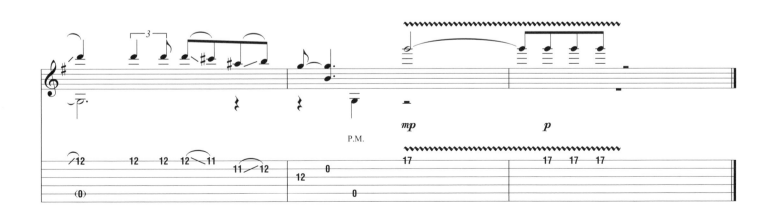

Sun's Gonna Shine in My Backdoor Someday Blues

Arranged by John Fahey

*Chord symbols reflect implied harmony.

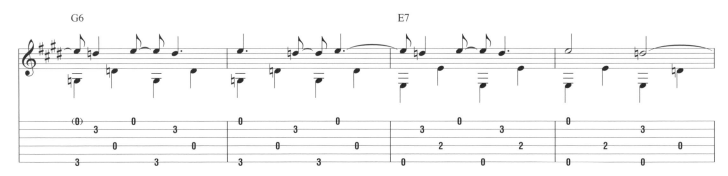

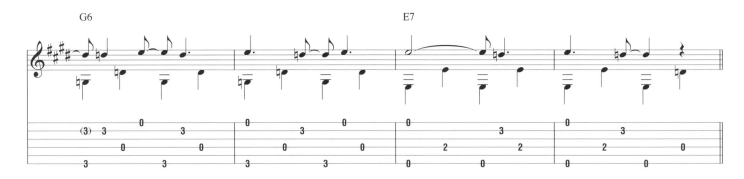

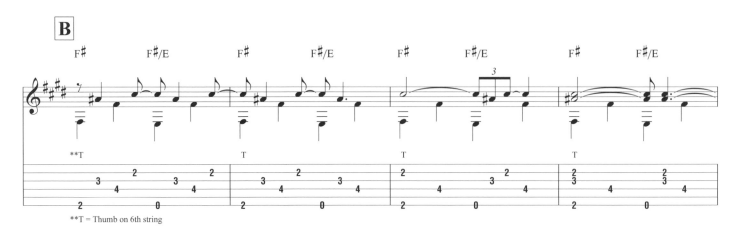

**T = Thumb on 6th string

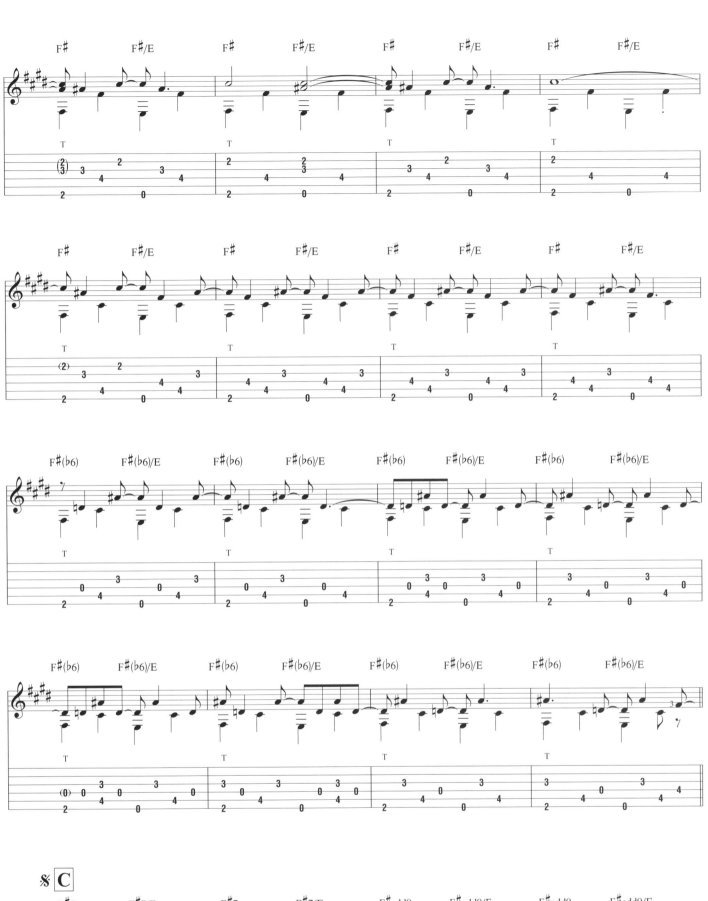

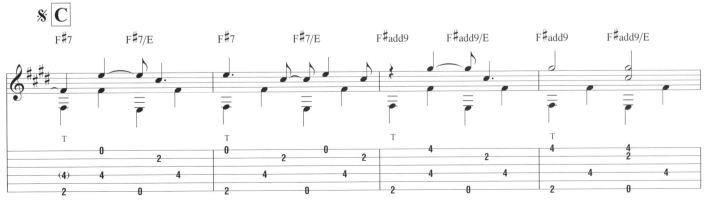

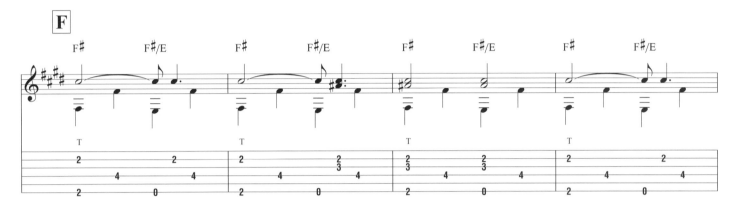

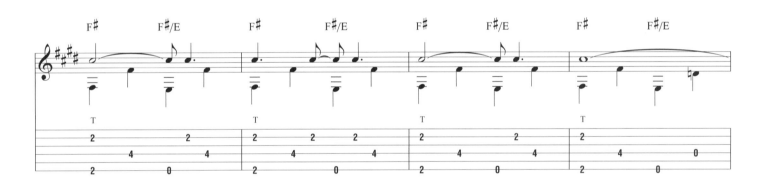

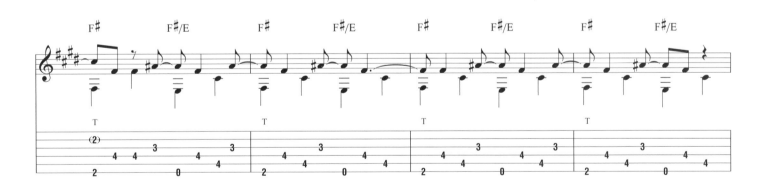

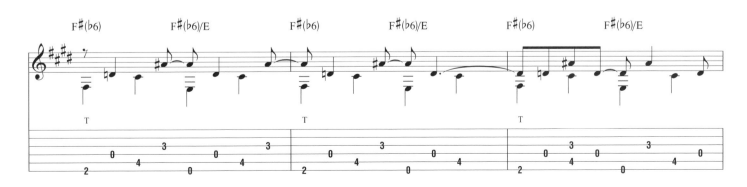

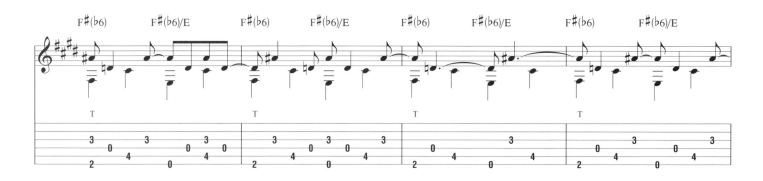

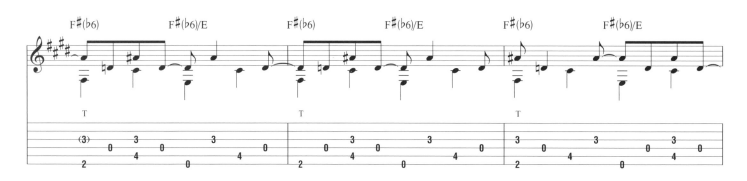

D.S. al Coda 1

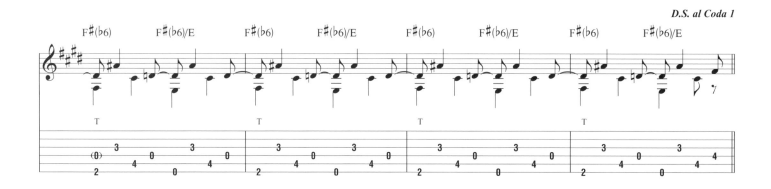

⊕ **Coda 1**

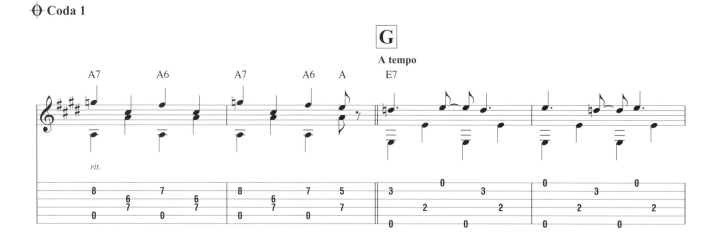

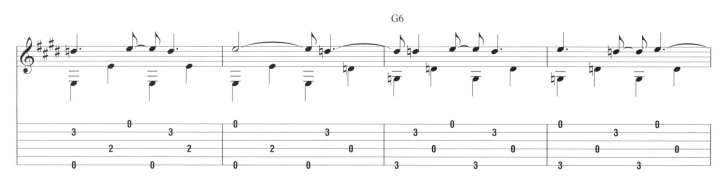

D.S. al Coda 2 $\oplus$ **Coda 2**

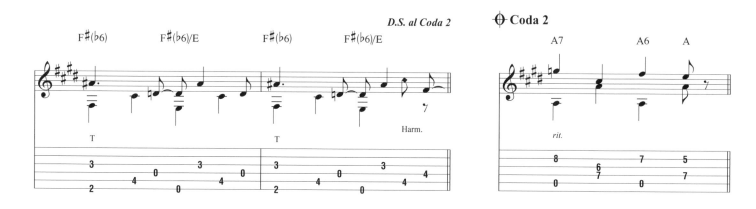

I

A tempo

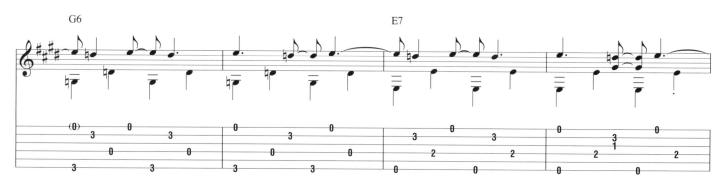

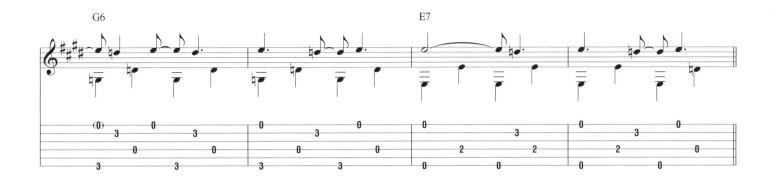

J

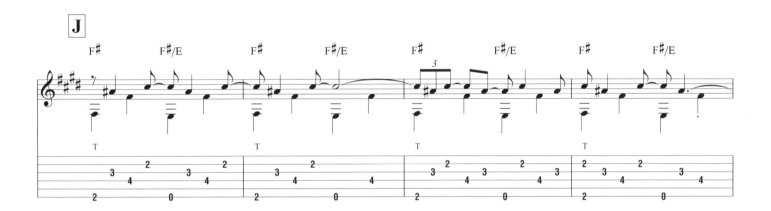

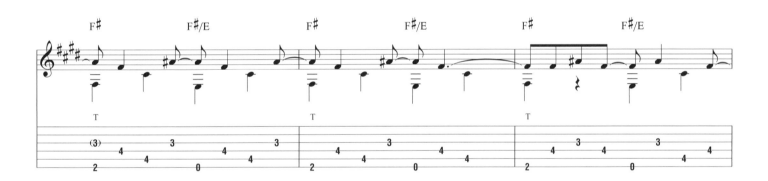

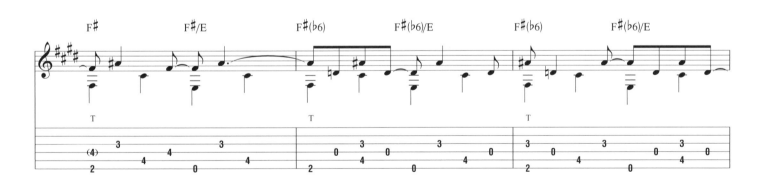

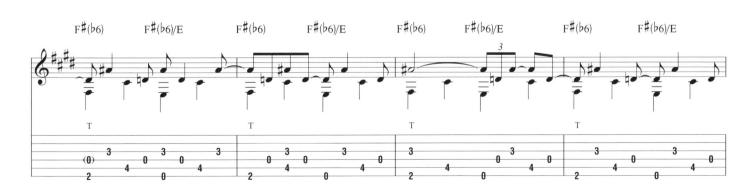

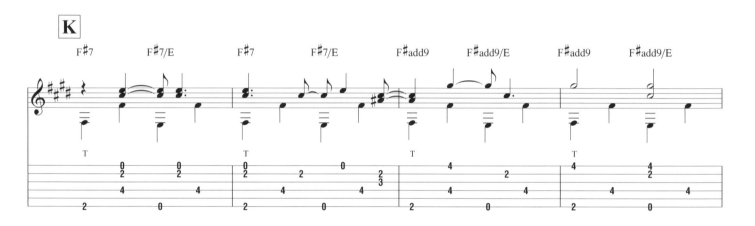

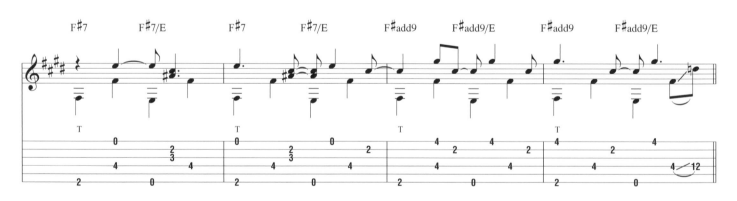

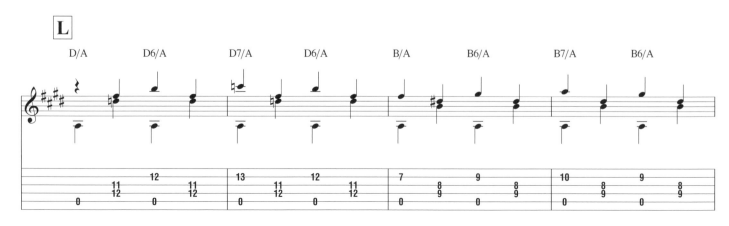

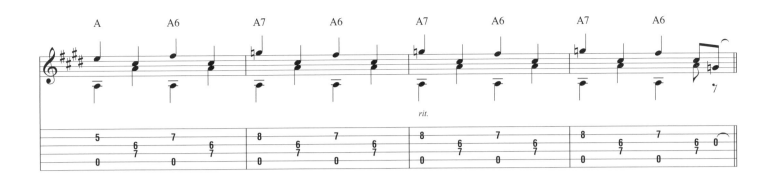

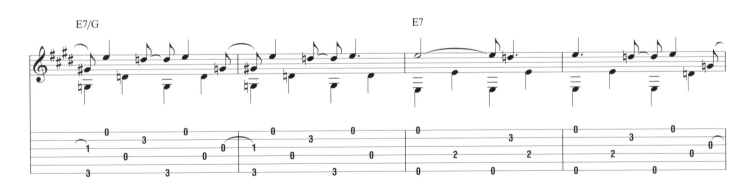

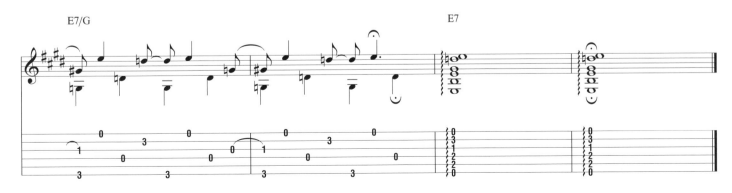

Sunflower River Blues

Written by John Fahey

Open C tuning:
(low to high) C-G-C-G-C-E

A

Free time

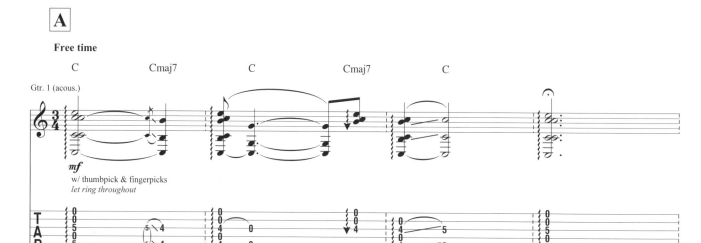

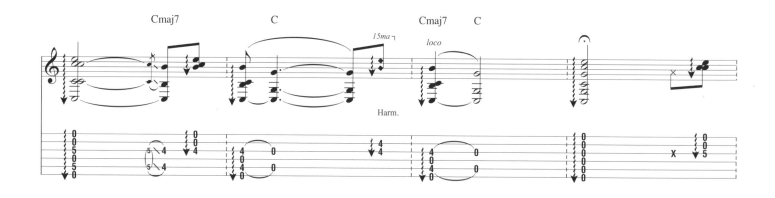

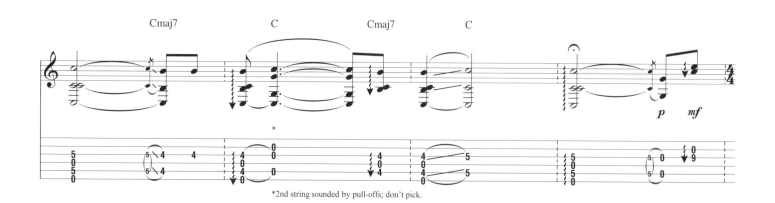

*2nd string sounded by pull-offs; don't pick.

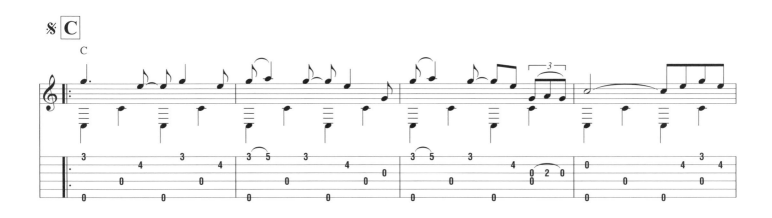

§ C

2nd time, Gtr. 1: w/ Fill 1

D

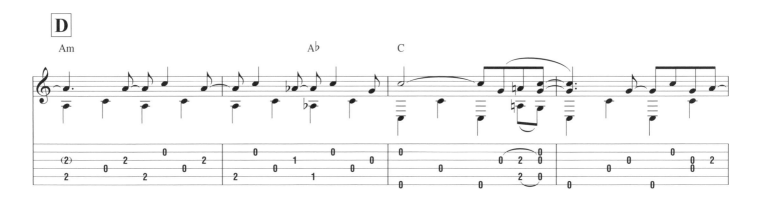

To Coda ⊕

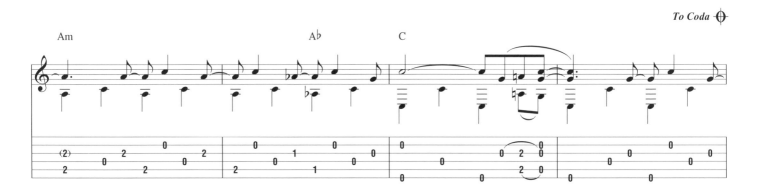

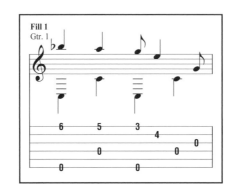

94

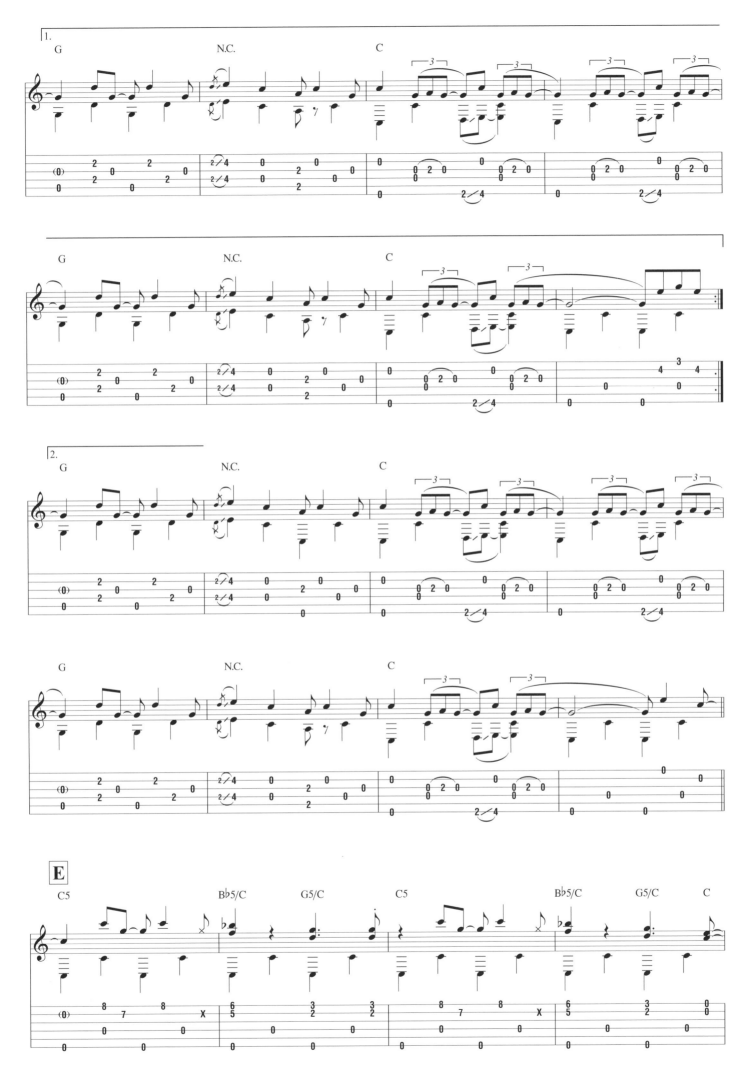

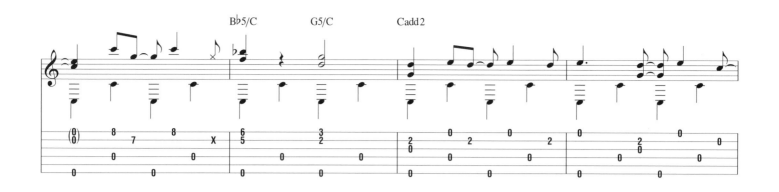

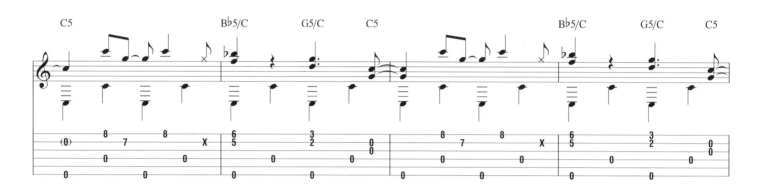

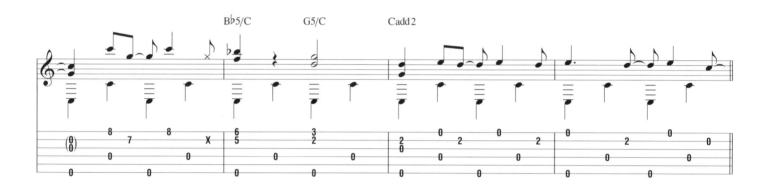

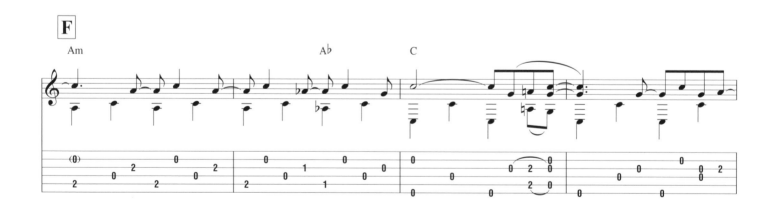

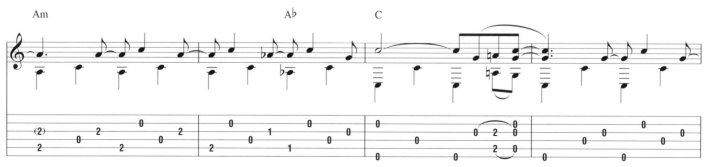

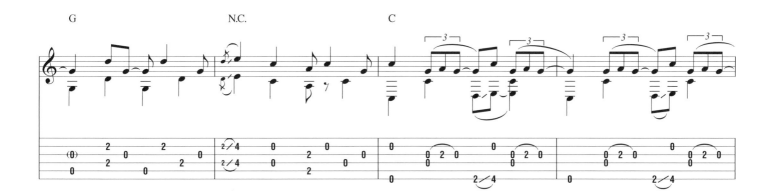

D.S. al Coda

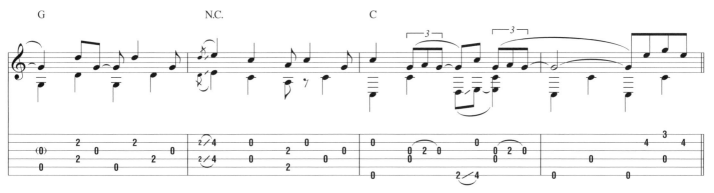

⊕ Coda

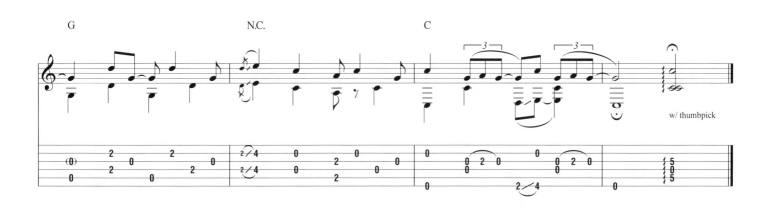

from *The Transfiguration of Blind Joe Death*

Tell Her to Come Back Home

Written by John Fahey

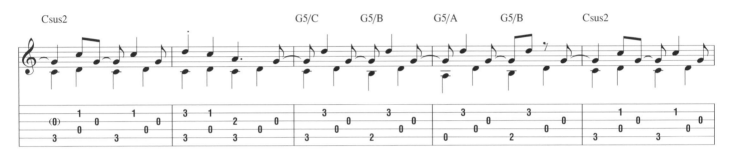

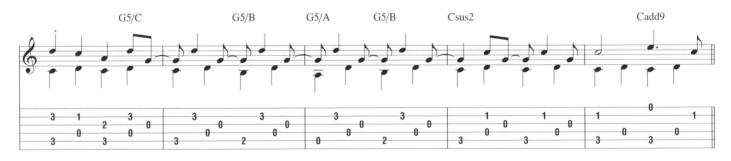

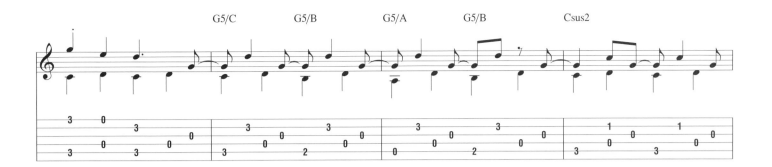

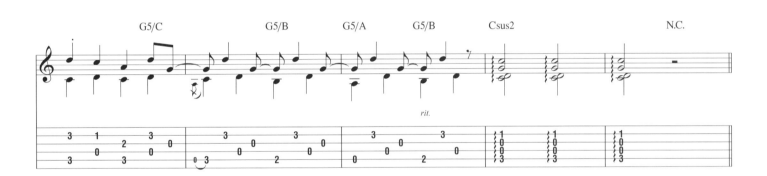

C

Tempo I

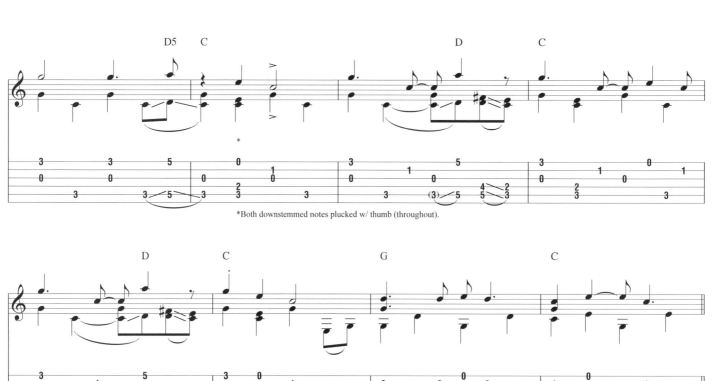

*Both downstemmed notes plucked w/ thumb (throughout).

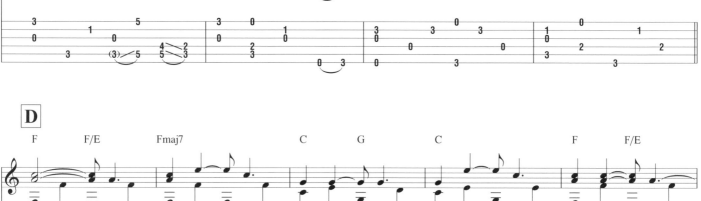

**T = Thumb on 6th string

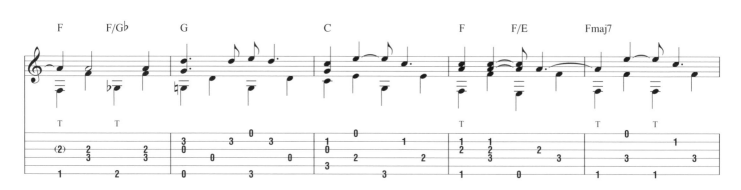

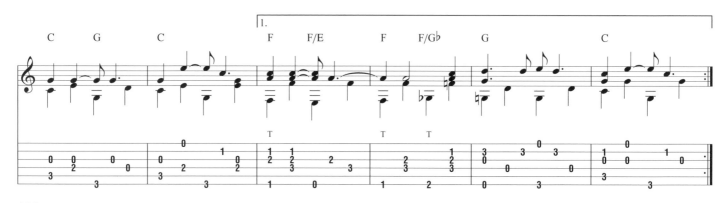

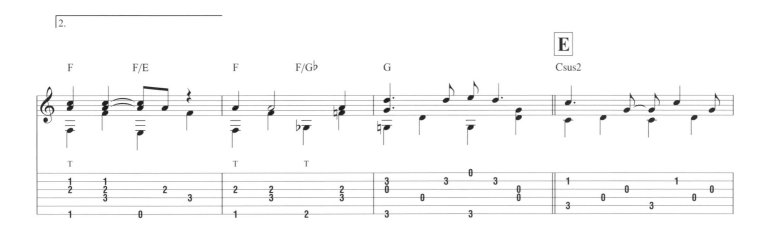

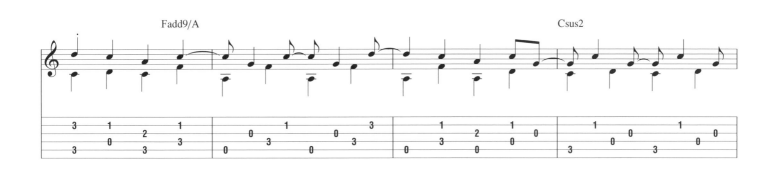

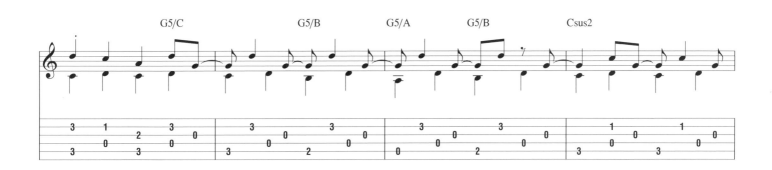

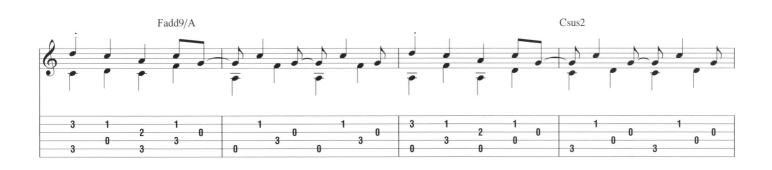

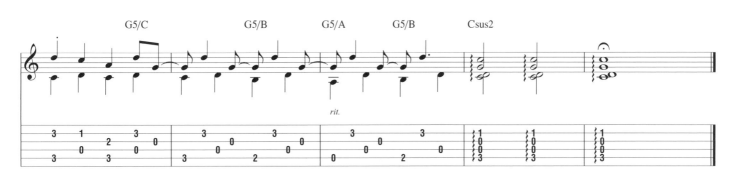

The Yellow Princess
Written by John Fahey

A

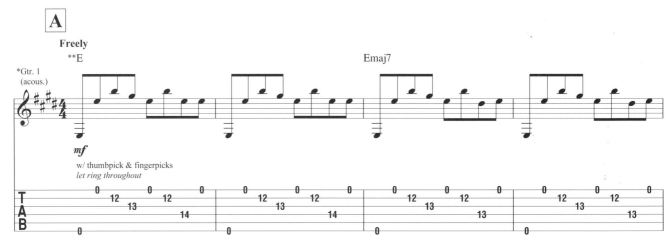

*To play along with recording, tune down 1/4 step.
**Chord symbols reflect implied harmony.

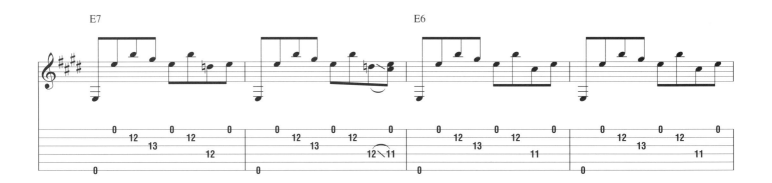

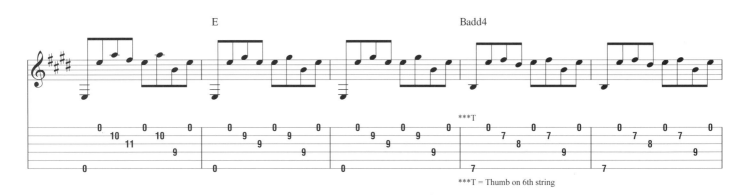

***T = Thumb on 6th string

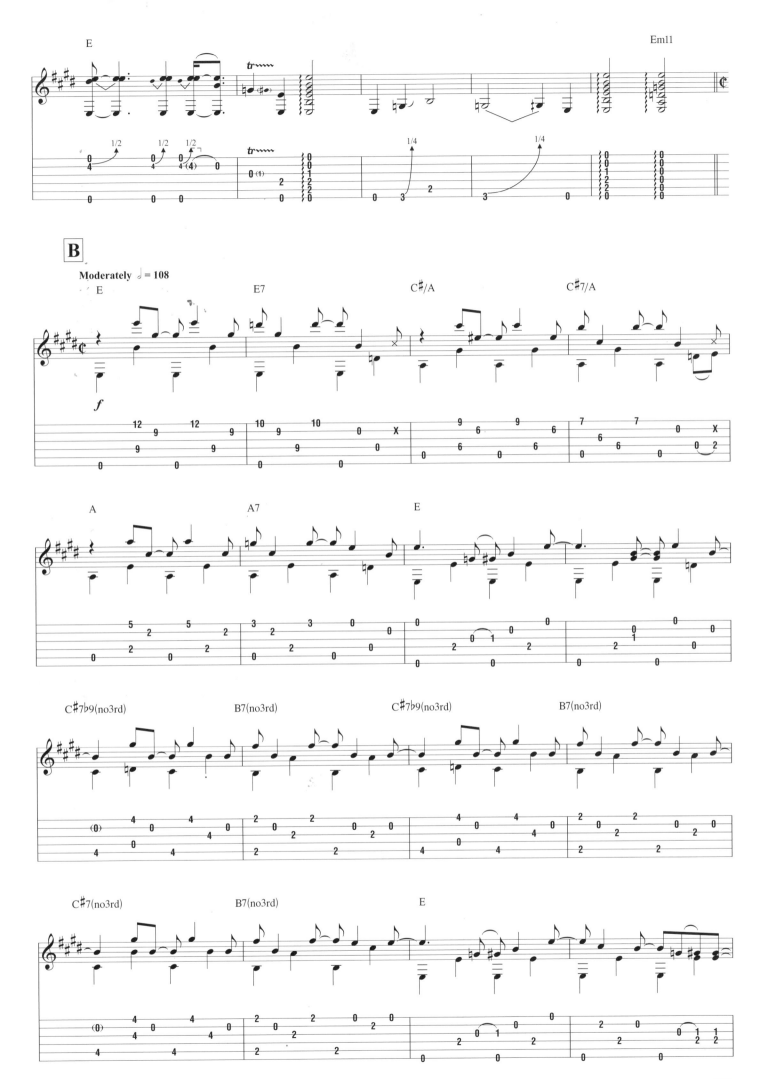

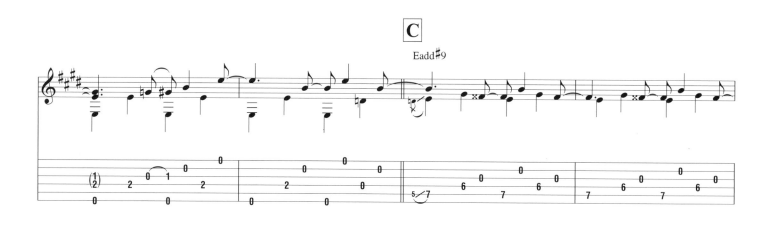

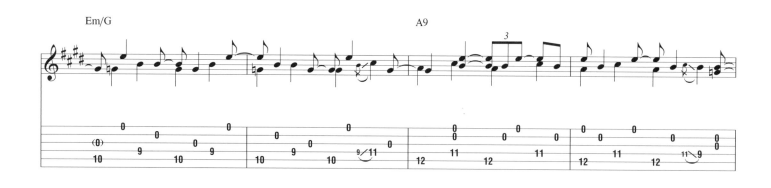

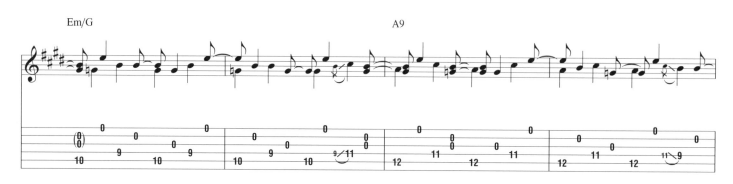

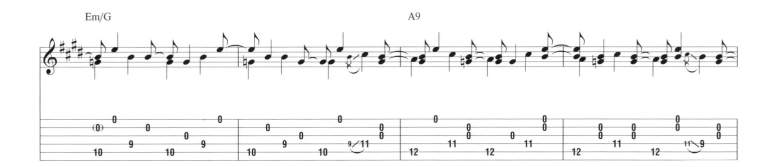

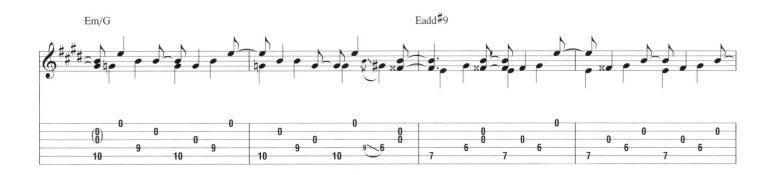

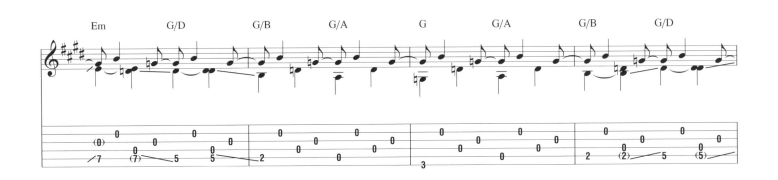

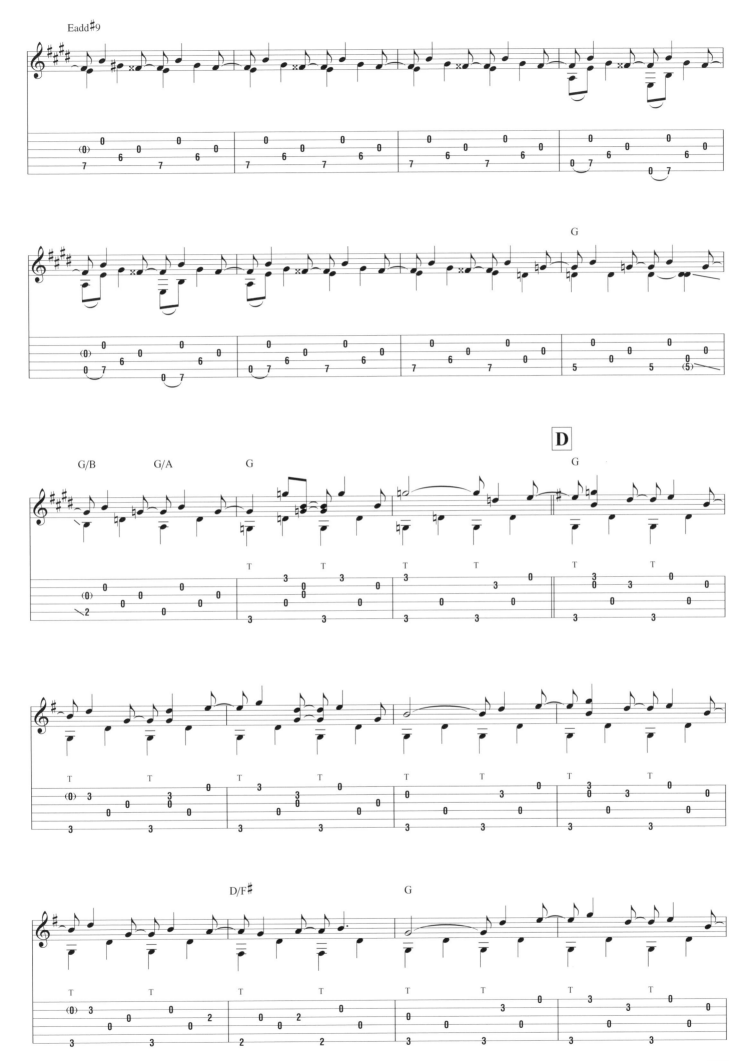

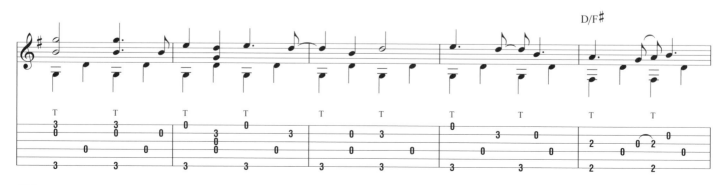

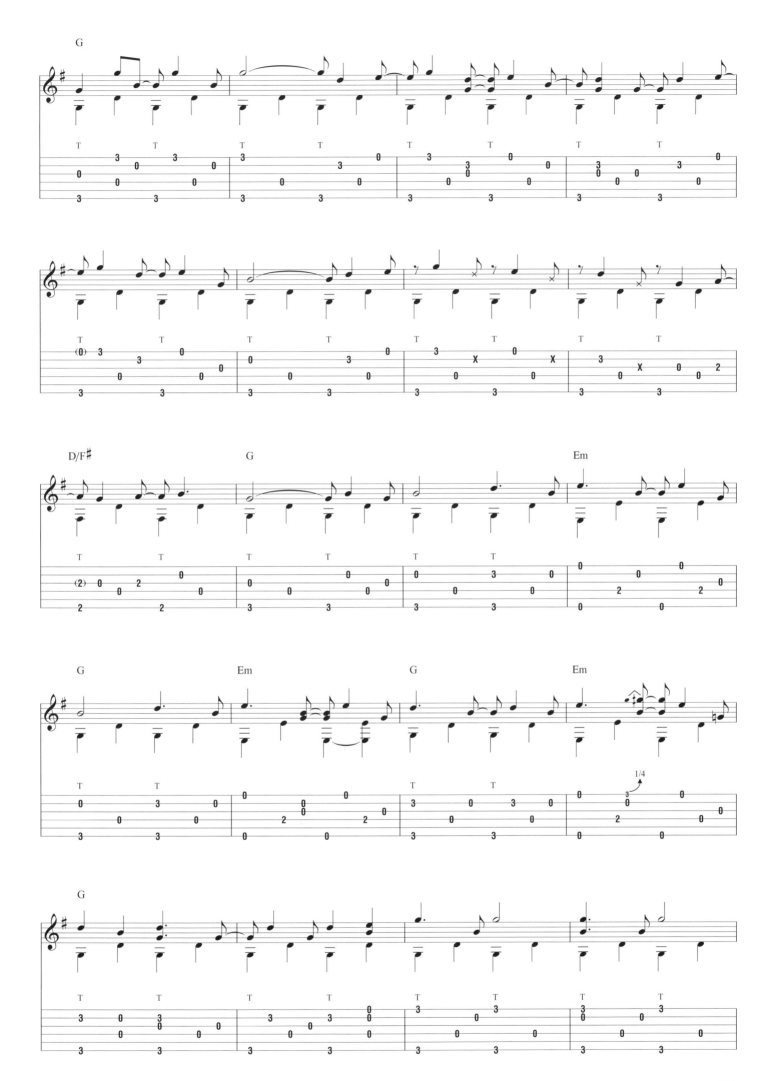

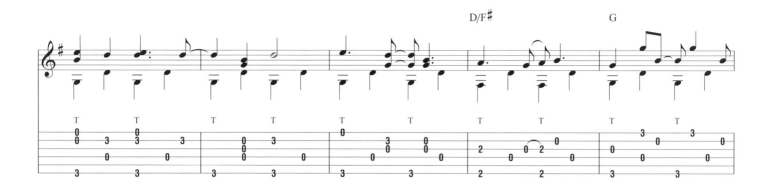

D/F#   G

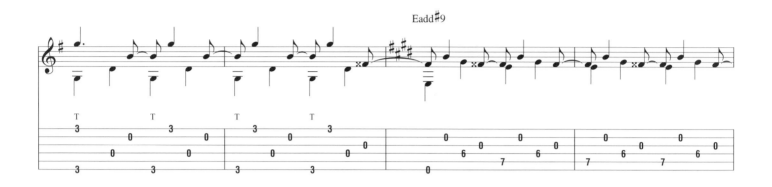

Eadd#9

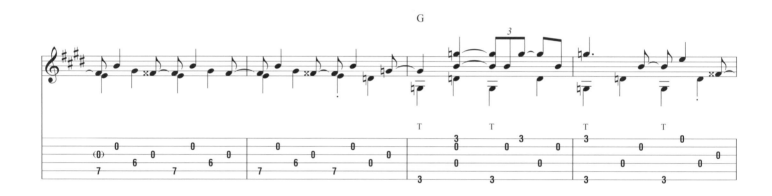

G

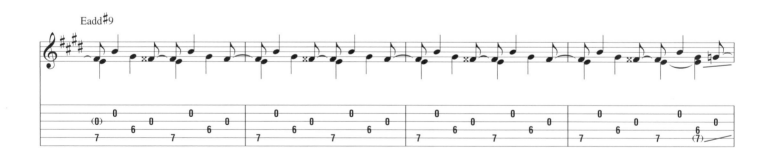

Eadd#9

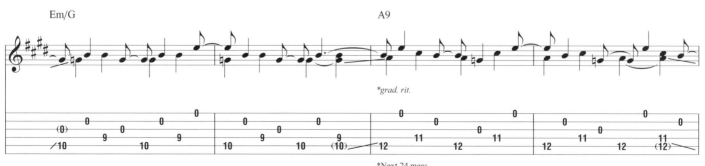

Em/G   A9

*grad. rit.

*Next 24 meas.

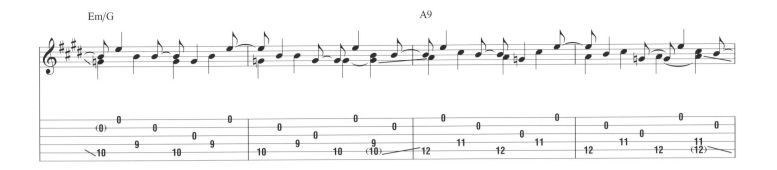

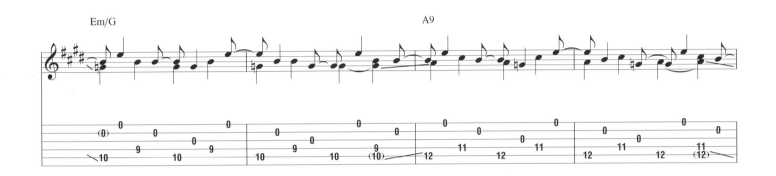

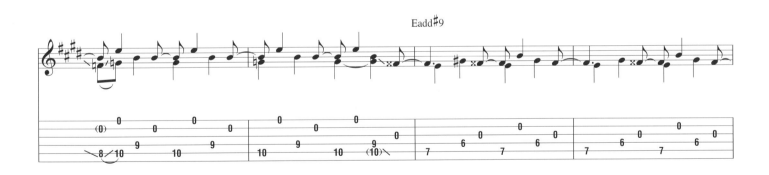

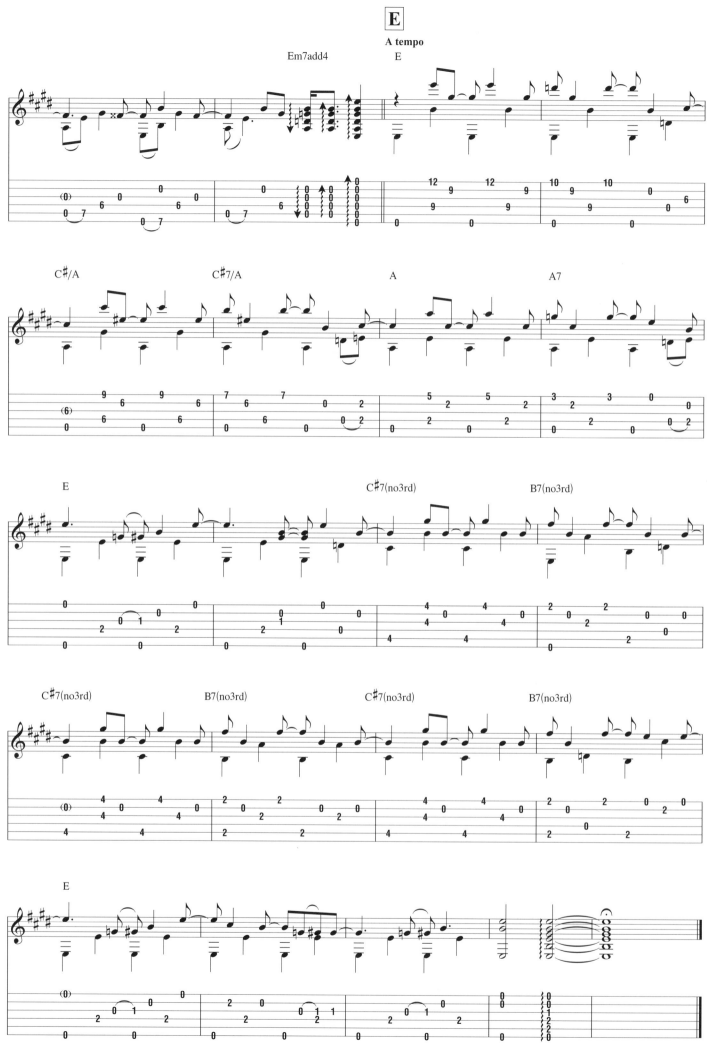